How to Play
The Torre Attack

Eric Schiller

Chess Digest, Inc.
1991

ISBN: 0-87568-199-9

Author: Eric Schiller
Manuscript preparation: Chessworks Unlimited
Typeset by M.L. Rantala in Adobe Hiroshige™ and Chessworks Unlimited's Gausdal Laserfont and Reykjavik Laserfont.
Cover: Elaine Smith
Proofreading: Hugh Myers
Publisher: Chess Digest, Inc., 1601 Tantor, Dallas, Texas, 75229.

Send the publisher $2 for the New Chess Guide that catalogs every book and chess item for general sale in the United States. You are given publishers, page counts, notation, diagram numbers, colors, and sizes of each item along with numerous pictures. Also included is a free Chess Improvement Course for beginners up through Master level.

Introduction and Historical Background

Carlos Torre (Mexico, 1904-1978) did not enjoy a long or particularly successful career in chess, but he did contribute significantly to opening theory by developing a plan involving d4, Nf3, and Bg5. In the 1920s, he stunned the chess world with a brilliant victory over Emanuel Lasker, and a quick kill against Saemisch, both at Moscow 1925. The variation is flexible, and allows both positional maneuvering and flashy gambit play.

The basic idea is similar to the Colle or the Stonewall Attack, in that White usually plays for a pawn structure with c3, d4, and e3. The difference is that in the Torre the Bc1 is allowed onto the battlefield immediately, instead of being entombed by pawns. Often it will pin a Black knight at f6, thus making the advance of a White pawn to e4 easier to achieve. Unlike the Trompowski (1.d4 Nf6 2.Bg5), the addition of 2.Nf3 for White takes the sting out of some of the plans with an early Qb6, since the d-pawn is overprotected.

Most of the World Champions have included the Torre Attack in their arsenal. For Alekhine, Spassky and Petrosian, it was a reliable weapon throughout their careers. One finds examples in the games of Capablanca, Botvinnik and Smyslov. Gary Kasparov has frequently resorted to it.

Others who reside on the Mt. Olympus of chess have used it effectively, including "vice-champions" Marshall, Keres, Bronstein, and Korchnoi. The great romantic Tartakower (who introduced the line against Saemisch at Vienna 1921) used it, as did the positional genius Nimzowitsch. The conservative Taimanov, the experimenter Basman, and the ever-creative Hort play the Torre, too.

In the contemporary arena, it is frequently employed by Eugene Torre (no relation), and young stars Yusupov, Salov, Dreyev, Yermolinsky, Piket and Hodgson.

Each variation is presented in the form of a complete game with notes so that typical opening strategies and middlegame ideas can be presented. The games are available in ChessBase™ and Access™ format. A companion database is available in Bookup7 format.

CONTENTS

CHAPTER ONE
1 d4 Nf6 2 Nf3 e6 3 Bg5

#1. HODGSON–KOSTEN
London (Nat West Young Masters), 1988

1 d4	Nf6
2 Nf3	e6
3 Bg5	

This is the basic starting position of the e6 line of the Torre Attack. White creates a pin which Black will have to deal with sooner or later.

3 ...	c5

Black strikes quickly at the White center, creating a tension which can last long into the middlegame. But the advantage of the Torre over most QP games is that White can support his central pawn with c2-c3 as well as e2-e3.

4 e3	

Now Black can choose from among many plans, of which 4...Be7 and 4...d5 are the most common.

4 ...	Be7
5 Nbd2	b6

This is the most principled continuation, since Black is not going to get the bishop developed along the c8-h3 diagonal. In addition, it puts more pressure on the critical central squares d5 and e4.

5...d6 6 Bd3 Nbd7 7 c3 a6 8 h3 b5 9 a4 Rb8 10 axb5 axb5 11 Qe2! c4 12 Bc2 Qc7 13 e4 is better for White, who dominates the center and the only open file, Schwarz - Kosikov, USSR Team Championship 1966.

5...cxd4 6 exd4 prematurely releases the tension in the center:

6...Nd5 7 Bxe7 Qxe7 8 c3 b6 9 g3! exploits the fact that Black determined the pawn structure before White had committed his bishop to d3. **9...0-0 10 Bg2 Ba6 11 c4! Nf6 12 0-0≠** Prokes - Vajda, Budapest 1929.

6 Bd3

6 ...   Bb7

6...Ba6?! 7 Bxf6 Bxf6 8 Ne4! Be7 9 d5! exd5 10 Bxa6 Nxa6 11 Qxd5 0-0 12 0-0 Nc7 13 Qd3 d5 14 Ng3 and White has excellent targets in the center and on the kingside, and will be able to mount pressure along the d-file, Van Scheltinga - Denker, Wijk aan Zee 1971.

7 0-0

This is the most solid continuation, since 7 c3 allows Black to try a number of alternatives to the main lines. In most cases, however, play will simply transpose. *7 c3 h6 (7...Nc6 8 Qe2?!* (Simply castling, transposing to the main lines, is better.) *8...cxd4 9 exd4 Nd5! 10 Bxe7 Ncxe7 11 g3 0-0 12 0-0 Ng6* and Black stood well in *Kholmov - Tal, USSR Championship 1959)* 8 Bh4 cxd4 9 exd4 g5 10 Bg3 Ng4 11 Ne5 h5 12 0-0 and now instead of 12...d6?, Klaman - Zhuravlev, Sevastopol 1976, Black should play 12...h4 13 Bf4 Rg8 with good attacking chances.

7 ...   0-0

a) 7...Nc6 8 c3 0-0 transposes to the main line.

b) 7...Nd5 8 Bxe7 Qxe7 9 c4 Nb4 10 Bb1 is much better for White since the knight will be driven away with tempo and the Black kingside is left without any defense at all.

c) 7...h6 8 Bh4 Nc6 *(8...d5?! 9 Ne5± - Gufeld)* 9 c3 0-0 10 Qe2 d5 11 dxc5 bxc5 12 e4 as suggested by Bellin, is better for White because he has strong pressure in the center and has completed his development. Black risks getting hanging pawns on the c- and d-files.

8 c3	Nc6

8...d6 brings about the "small center" formation favored by Andersson 9 Re1 cxd4 10 exd4 Nbd7 11 a4 (11 Qb3!?) a6 12 b4?! h6 13 Bh4 Nd5 14 Bxe7 Qxe7 gave Black a good game in Larsen - Andersson, Biel Interzonal 1976.

9 a3!?

An interesting plan, motivated by the fact that slow approaches don't achieve anything:

a) 9 Re1 Rc8 10 Rc1 (*10 dxc5 bxc5 11 e4!?* is suggested by Bellin) Nh5! A liberating maneuver which assures equality. 11 Ne4 f6! 12 Bh4 g6 and despite the odd-looking pawn structure, Black has a fine game, Balashov - Miles, Novi Sad 1975.

b) 9 Qe2 cxd4 10 cxd4 Nd5 11 Bxe7 Ncxe7 was fine for Black in Krasnov - Averkin, USSR 1969, similar to the Kholmov - Tal game cited above.

9 ...	cxd4
10 exd4	Nd5
11 Bxe7	Ncxe7
12 Re1	

What has White achieved to this point? He has control of most of the center, and potential kingside attacks. Black addresses both points on his next move.

12 ...	f5
13 c4	Nf4
14 Bf1!	

With the kingside attack no longer a reasonable plan, this is the proper post for the bishop.

14 ...	Rf6
15 Qb3	Rh6

Black is making threatening moves on the kingside, but it is well defended and the long range bishop can be cut off with a timely d4–d5.

16	Rad1	g5
17	d5!	g4

17...exd5 18 Nxg5!? Rg6 19 Ndf3 h6 20 Qe3 Ne6 21 Nxe6 dxe6 22 Ne5 looks promising for White.

18	Nd4	Neg6

This gives up a pawn, but there was little choice.

19	dxe6	dxe6
20	Nxe6	Nxe6
21	Rxe6	

Black is busted here, unl.ess he can whip up a decisive kingside attack.

21	...	Qh4
22	h3	Rd8

22...gxh3 23 Qxh3 Qf4 24 Qg3 puts an end to the attack.

23	c5!	

Now White has regained the initiative.

23	...	Bd5
24	Bc4	Bxe6
25	Bxe6+	Kg7
26	c6	

The exchange sacrifice has led to the establishment of a powerful passed pawn.

26	...	Ne7
27	c7	Rf8
28	Re1!	

A subtle move which increases the pressure and supports the Be6 so that the queen is free for other tasks.

28 ...	gxh3
29 Nf3	Qf6
30 Bd7	hxg2
31 Re6	Qf7

Or 31...Rh1+ 32 Kxg2+-.

32 Qc3+	Rf6
33 Ng5	Qh5
34 Rxe7+	Kg6
35 Nh3	Qd1+
36 Kxg2	Kh6

Finally the lines are open, but it is too late.

37 Qe5	Rg6+
38 Kh2	f4
39 c8Q	resigns

#2. YERMOLINSKY–NAUMKIN
Tashkent, 1987

1 d4	Nf6
2 Nf3	e6
3 Bg5	c5
4 e3	d5

In this variation Black aims for a strong presence in the center.

5 Nbd2	Nc6

Although this move seems logical, the knight is not really well-placed here.

6 c3	Qb6

a) 6...cxd4 7 exd4 Bd6 (7...Be7 8 Bd3 h6 9 Bf4 Nh5 10 Be3! Nf6 11 Ne5 Nxe5 12 dxe5 Nd7 13 Bd4! gave White tremendous pressure in *Petrosian - Mecking, Wijk aan Zee 1971)* 8 Bd3 h6 9 Bh4≠.

b) 6...Be7 7 Bd3 h6 8 Bh4 Nd7 9 Bg3! The retreat is clearly better than the exchange. 9...0-0 10 Qe2 c4 11 Bc2 f5 The only way to stop e4. 12 h4! b5 13 e4! and White has achieved a decisive breakthrough, as seen in Kholmov - Tseshkovsky, USSR Championship 1969. The point is that if Black takes at e4 White simply sacs the knight and recaptures with the queen.

c) 6...Bd6!? is possible.

7 Bxf6

7 Qb3 Be7 8 Be2 0-0 9 0-0 Re8 10 Rad1 cxd4 11 exd4 Ne4 12 Bxe7 Nxd2 13 Rxd2 Rxe7 14 Bd3 was slightly better for White in Trifunovic - Averbakh, USSR vs Yugoslavia, 1961.

7 ...	gxf6
8 Rb1	

White has a very comfortable game.

8 ...	e5
9 e4	cxd4
10 exd5	Ne7
11 cxd4	Nxd5
12 Bc4	

White maintains the pressure and keeps the initiative, since Black cannot retreat to b6 because the queen occupies that square.

12 ...	Be6
13 Rc1	exd4
14 0-0	

The weak Pd4 can be regained later.

14 ...	Bh6
15 Bxd5	Bxd5

16 Nc4!

Breaking the pin with style!

16 ...   Qd8
17 Rc2   b5

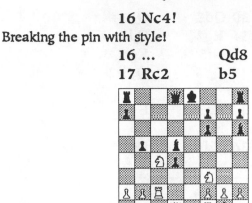

18 Re1+!

An important zwischenzug.

18 ...   Kf8
19 Ncd2   Qd7
20 Ne4   Bxe4
21 Rxe4

And the Pd4 is encircled, while White dominates the central files.

21 ...   d3
22 Rc3   d2
23 Rd4   Qe6
24 Nxd2   Qxa2
25 Ne4

The weakness of the Black king is much more important than the pawn.

25 ...   Re8
26 Rd8   Qe6
27 Rxe8+   Kxe8
28 Nd6+   Kf8
29 g3

Not only does this create luft, it also threatens to excommunicate the Black bishop, which is disastrous considering that the Rh8 is also unable to enter the game.

29...   Kg7

30 Qd3	Qe1+
31 Kg2	Qd2
32 Nf5+!	Kg6
33 Qe4	Qxb2

There was nothing better.

34 Rc5	Bg5
35 h4	h6
36 Nd4+	Kg7

37 Ne6+!	resigns.

#3. PIKET–KAROLYI
Brussels, 1987

1 d4	d5
2 Nf3	Nf6
3 Bg5	e6
4 e3	c5
5 Nbd2	Qb6

An aggressive move, but one which leads to a structural weakness for Black.

6 Bxf6	gxf6

Black will have to prove that there is some compensation for the weaknesses on the kingside.

7 c4!   cxd4

7...Qxb2 8 cxd5 exd5 9 Rb1 Qxa2 10 Bb5+ Nc6 11 dxc5 ± was demonstrated long ago by Tolush.

8 exd4   dxc4
9 Bxc4   Bg7

9...Nc6 10 0-0 Bd7 (10...Nxd4? 11 Ne4 Nxf3+ 12 Qxf3 f5 13 Qc3 fxe4 14 Qxh8 Bd7 15 Qxh7 leaves Black without any compensation) 11 d5 exd5 (11...Na5?! 12 Rc1 e5 13 Qe2 Bg7 14 Bd3 Qxb2 15 Rc2 Qb6 16 Rb1 Qd6 17 Ne4 and Black was busted in Tolush - Flohr, Parnu 1947) 12 Qe2+ Ne7 13 Bxd5 gave White a clear advantage in Spassky - Zaitsev, USSR Championship 1963.

10 0-0   0-0
11 Re1   Rd8

12 d5!   Na6

12...exd5 13 Bxd5 Rxd5 14 Re8+ Bf8 15 Rxc8 is clearly unpleasant for Black.

13 dxe6   fxe6
14 Qe2

The weakness of Black's pawn structure is critical, even without taking into account White's lead in development.

14 ...   Nc7
15 Nf1   Bd7
16 Ng3   Re8
17 Rad1   Bc6
18 Nd4

Every one of White's moves is dedicated to improving the placement of his pieces and securing his position in the center.

Black, on the other hand, is just trying to get his pieces untied.

18 ...	Bd5	
19 Nh5!	Bxc4	
20 Qxc4	Kh8	
21 Rc1!	Rac8	

22 Nf5!!

Effectively exploiting Black's overworked major pieces.

22 ...	exf5
23 Rxe8+	Rxe8
24 Qf7	

But not 24 Qxc7?? Qxc7 25 Rxc7 Re1#.

24...	Rg8
25 Rxc7	resigns.

#4. MOHR–ANAND
Belgrade, 1988

1 d4 d5 2 Nf3 Nf6 3 Bg5 e6 4 e3 c5 5 Nbd2 Nbd7 6 c3 Be7 7 Bd3

This is a very reasonable formation for Black, provided that he follows up consistently.

7 ...	b6

a) 7...0-0 looks good, but allows White to establish a strong outpost at e5. 8 Ne5 (The most accurate move, although White can also simply castle, as in Schiller - Rokop, Bradford 1991, which continued 8 0-0 Qc7 9 Qe2 b6 10 Bf4 Bd6 11 Bxd6 Qxd6 12 e4! to which Black should have replied 12....dxe4 13 Nxe4 Qe7 14 dxc5 Nxc5 15 Nxc5 Qxc5 16 Rad1 Bb7 although after 17 Ba6! White would have enjoyued a clear advantage. Instead, Black played 12...e5?! and after 13 dxe5 Nxe5 14 Nxe5 Qxe5 15 f4 Qe7?! ran into 16 e5 Nd7 17 c4! where the best Black could do would have been 17...Bb7 18 cxd5 Bxd5 19 Bxh7+ Kxh7 20 Qd3+ Kg8 21 Qxd5 ±. But Black, unaware of the danger, played 17...d4?, and resigned after 18 Qe4.) 8...Nxc5 9 dxc5 Nd7 10 Bf4! f5 11 h4 c4 12 Bc2 b5 13 Nf3 Nc5 14 g4! b4 15 gxf5 exf5 16 Ng5 gave White an overwhelming position in Petrosian - Lyublinsky, USSR Championship 1949.

b) 7...h6 8 Bf4 0-0 9 Ne5 Qb6 10 Rb1! cxd4 11 exd4 Nxe5 12 dxc5 Nd7 13 Qg4 proved decisive in Averkin - Galdanov, Riazan 1975.

8 Ne5!

This is more to the point than prosaic castling.

8 ...   Bb7

8...Nxe5 9 dxe5 Nd7 10 Bxe7 Qxe7 11 f4 is evaluated by Bellin as equal, but there are good reasons to prefer White here. The Black center can come under attack with e4 or c4, and White can also attack on the kingside: 11...Bb7 12 0-0 0-0-0 (12...0-0 13 Qh5 g6 14 Qf3 Rab8 15 e4±) 13 a4 g5 14 a5 gxf4 15 exf4 Rdg8 16 axb6 axb6 17 Ba6 followed by an exchange of bishops and b2-b4 gives White the more dangerous initiative.

9 f4	0-0
10 Qf3!	h6

Now Black probably expected the bishop to retreat, after which his game would not be too bad, but White has a more aggressive possibility.

> 11 h4   Ne8

11...hxg5 12 hxg5 Ne8 13 Bh7+ Kh8 14 Bg6+ Kg8 15 Rh8+ Kxh8 16 Qh5+ Kg8 17 Qh7 mate would have been a pretty finish.

> 12 Bxh6!

White is determined to sacrifice the piece and expose the enemy king.

> 12...   gxh6
> 13 Qh5   f5

Black needs to create some breathing room and keep the White pieces out of the game.

> 14 g4

The natural response. No need to capture at h6 just yet.

> 14 ...   Ng7
> 15 Qxh6   Rf6
> 16 Ng6

White now threatens g4-g5, so...

> 16 ...   Rxg6
> 17 Qxg6   Nf8
> 18 Qh6

Despite the lack of maneuvering room, there is no way for Black to trap the queen.

> 18 ...   fxg4
> 19 0-0-0

White now has a decisive advantage on the kingside.

> 19 ...   Nf5
> 20 Qh5   Nxe3
> 21 Rde1   cxd4

Black is finally going to get some counterplay by cracking open the queenside, or so he thinks!

	22 Rxe3!	dxe3
	23 Qxg4+	Kf7
	24 Qh5+	

There will be no escape to the center!

	24 ...	Kf6
	25 Qe5+	Kf7
	26 Qh5+	Kf6
	27 Nf3	Bd6

Otherwise Ne5 will be terminal, e.g., 27...d4 28 Ne5 Bxh1 29 Qf7+#.

	28 Qh6+	Ke7
	29 Qg7+	Ke8
	30 Bb5+	Nd7
	31 Ng5	Qe7
	32 Qg8+	resigns.

#5. YERMOLINSKY–BANDZA
USSR, 1987

1 d4 Nf6 2 Nf3 e6 3 Bg5 c5 4 e3 d5 5 Nbd2 Nbd7 6 c3 Qc7 7 Bd3 b6

This formation is intended to prevent Ne5, but Yermolinsky introduces a bold new plan.

8 Ne5	Nxe5
9 dxe5	Qxe5
10 Bf4	Qh5
11 Bb5+	Bd7
12 Bxd7+	Kxd7
13 Qa4+	Kd8

This is all pretty much forced. The Black queen is offside and will not be able to help with the defense, while all White needs is his active pieces.

14 Nf3!

Intending Ne5.

14 ...	Nd7
15 Rd1!	

White displays appropriate patience. His other forces are well-deployed, and now the big artillery is moved into position.

15 ...	f6
16 Qc6	Rc8
17 Qxe6	

Now the move of the rook to the d-file is shown to be logical.

17 ...   Qe8
18 Qxd5   g5

White has an extra pawn and Black's pieces are helpless. The King is just begging for a fancy mating attack. Yermolinsky obliges.

19 Bxg5!!   fxg5
20 Nxg5 Qe7

20...Bg7 21 Ne6+.

21 Nf7+   Ke8
22 Nxh8   Nf6
23 Qf5!   Rc7
24 0-0

White is still in no hurry, now that he has an overwhelming material advantage. Black could resign here with a clear conscience.

24...   Bg7
25 Ng6   hxg6
26 Qxg6+   Kf8
27 Rd3   Rc8
28 Rfd1   Kg8
29 e4   Rf8
30 Rg3   Ne8
31 Rd5   Rf6
32 Qg4   Re6
33 e5   resigns.

#6. YUSUPOV–KARPOV
London, 5th match game, 1989
1 d4 Nf6 2 Nf3 e6 3 Bg5 c5 4 e3 b6

This has long been considered to be a weak move, because White can reply 5 d5! which exploits the pin effectively.

5 d5!   exd5

a) 5...h6 6 Bxf6 Qxf6 7 Nc3 a6 8 a4 d6 9 Nd2! e5 10 Bd3 Qd8 11 0-0 with an obvious advantage for White, who is well-developed and controls the center, Petrosian - Peterson, USSR Team Championship 1960.

b) 5...d6 It is interesting to note that Yusupov has considerable experience in the line as evidenced by the following continuation: 6 dxe6 Bxe6 7 Bb5+ Nbd7 8 Nc3 a6 9 Bxd7+ Bxd7 10 Nd5 Be7 11 Bxf6 Bxf6 12 Nxf6+ Qxf6 13 Qd5 ± Yusupov - Frisnielsen, Skien 1979.

c) 5...b5!? is an interesting line used effectively by Speelman against Cifuentes at the 1980 Malta Olympiad. But objectively, the waste of tempo cannot be justified - see the lines with an early c5 and b5 for Black. 6 Nc3 (*6 Bxb5? Qa5+ 7 Nc3 Ne4∓*) a6 and now instead of the boring 7 a4, White might have tried either 7 e4 or Ne4.

6 Nc3   Be7

6...Bb7 7 Nxd5 Bxd5 8 Bxf6 Qxf6 9 Qxd5 is clearly better for White. 9...Nc6 (*9...Qxb2? 10 Rd1! Qb4+ 11 c3! Qxc3+ 12 Rd2 Qc1+ 13 Ke2* and Black is busted.) 10 0-0-0 Rd8 11 Bb5 Be7 12 Bxc6 dxc6 13 Qe5± Bronstein - Foguelman, Mar del Plata 1960.

7 Nxd5   Bb7
8 Bxf6   Bxf6
9 c3

White stands better, thanks to the outpost at d5.

9 ...	0-0
10 Bc4	a6
11 0-0	b5
12 Bb3	d6
13 Qd2	

White has a clear target at d6, and the Bb3 can operate on either the a2-g8 or b1-h7 diagonals.

13 ...	Nd7
14 Rfd1	Bxd5
15 Bxd5	Rb8
16 Qc2!	

A clever move with two purposes. It threatens Be4 with threats at d6 and h7, and at the same time sets up a man-to-man coverage between the Rd1 and Qd8.

16 ...	Nb6
17 Rd2	g6
18 Rad1	Qc7

White has an excellent game here, and he had only to continue with the logical attacking move 19 h4! to have excellent winning chances.

19 Qe4?!	Kg7
20 h4	Qe7!

Karpov threatens to slow the attack by offering an exchange of queens while putting pressure on the Ph4.

21 Qf4	Be5!

This is actually a bad bishop, and Karpov is only too glad to be rid of it.

22 Nxe5	dxe5
23 Qg3	Rbd8
24 h5	Rd7

24...Rd6? 25 hxg6 hxg6? 26 Bxf7! ±.

25 b3	Rfd8
26 e4	g5?

There was no need to create this additional weakness. (26... c4!?)

27 Qe3	h6
28 c4!	Rc7
29 Rd3	Nd7?

Keeping in mind the variation discussed earlier, Black would have done well to leave the knight where it was.

30 Bxf7!!	Kxf7
31 Qd2	Ke8
32 Qa5	bxc4
33 bxc4?!	

33 Rd6! cxb3 34 Qxa6 bxa2 35 Re6.

33 ...	Rcc8?

In extreme time trouble, the play gets sloppy. Better 33...Rc6 34 Rd5 Qe6 35 Qd2±.

34 Qa4	Rc7

35 Qxa6	Rb8
36 Qg6+	Kf8
37 Rf3+	resigns.

#7. C.TORRE–EM.LASKER
Moscow, 1925

1 d4 Nf6 2 Nf3 e6 3 Bg5 c5 4 e3 cxd4

This exchange may be thought to be premature, but in fact it will usually transpose to normal lines.

5 exd4	Be7
6 Nbd2	d6
7 c3	Nbd7
8 Bd3	b6

Black has chosen a solid formation, but Torre was getting a lot of practice in these lines in 1925!

9 Nc4

Torre was fond of this maneuver, though there is no need to rush. An alternative is 9 0-0 0-0 10 Re1 Bb7 11 Nc4, which is perhaps a more reliable move order.

9 ...	Bb7
10 Qe2	Qc7
11 0-0	0-0

Both sides have continued with the logical development of their ideas. White has intensified the pressure on the center, and Black has dug in.

> **12 Rfe1 Rfe8**
> **13 Rad1**

Leading up to this point I have seen several different move orders for the game.

> **13 ...**   **Nf8**
> **14 Bc1**   **Nd5**
> **15 Ng5?!**

15 Na3 was more logical, preventing Black's liberating maneuver.

> **15 ...**   **b5!**
> **16 Na3**

16 Ne3? Bxg5 17 Nxd5 exd5! 18 Qg4 Bxc1 19 Rxc1 Ng6=.

> **16 ...**   **b4**
> **17 cxb4**   **Nxb4**
> **18 Qh5?!**

18 Bb1 was the more conservative and logical choice.

> **18 ...**   **Bxg5**
> **19 Bxg5**

19 Qxg5!? Nxa2 20 Bd2 a5 21 Ra1 Nb4 22 Bxb4 axb4 23 Nb5 Qc6 24 Rac1 Qb6 25 Re3 is an interesting alternative.

> **19 ...**   **Nxd3**
> **20 Rxd3 Qa5!**

A clever defensive move, attacking the Re1 while pinning the Bg5. Without a light-squared bishop, White is going to have to work hard to whip up an attack...

> **21 b4!?**   **Qf5?!**

a) 21...Qxb4?! 22 Rb1 Qa5 23 Nc4 Qa6 24 Rxb7!? Qxb7 25 Nxd6 Qd7 26 Nxe8 Qxe8 27 h3 with a very slight advantage for White.

b) 21...Qd5! would have been best, with severe problems for White, e.g., 22 Qf3 (22 Rg3 h6 23 Bf6 Ng6! 24 Rxg6 fxg6 25 Qxg6 Qxg2+! 26 Qxg2 Bxg2 27 Bxg7! Kxg7 28 Kxg2 with some drawing chances for White. Or 22 Qg4 e5!∓) 22...Rab8! 23 Bf4 Qf5! 24 Qg3 e5 25 dxe5 Ng6 26 Bc1 Nxe5 27 Rdd1 Re6 28 Qf4 Qg6 29 Qg3 Rbe8 30 Qxg6 (30 Kf1 Qh5 -+) 30...Nf3+ 31 gxf3 Rxe1+ 32 Rxe1 Rxe1+ 33 Kg2 hxg6 34 Bf4 Ra1 35 Bxd6 Rxa2 36 Nc4 Rc2∓]

22 Rg3   h6

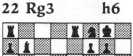

23 Nc4!

In order for an attack to be successful, all of the pieces must get into the act!

23 ...   Qd5?

Lasker should have accepted the challenge with 23...hxg5 24 Nxd6 Qg6 25 Qxg6 Nxg6 26 Nxb7 Rab8 27 Nc5 Rxb4 28 Rxg5 Nf4! and Black is no worse.

24 Nc3   Qb5

24...Qxd4? 25 Rd1! Qb2 (25...Qxb4 26 Bf6 g6 27 Qxh6+–) 26 Bxh6 Ng6 27 Bg5 with Rh3 to follow.

25 Bf6!!   Qxh5

26 Rxg7+   Kh8

27 Rxf7+   Kg8

28 Rg7+   Kh8

29 Rxb7+   Kg8

30 Rg7+   Kh8

31 Rg5+   Kh7

32 Rxh5   Kg6

33 Rh3	Kxf6
34 Rxh6+	Kg5
35 Rh3	

The carnage is complete and White has an easy win in the endgame.

| 35... | Reb8 |

36 Rg3+ Kf6 37 Rf3+ Kg6 38 a3 a5 39 bxa5 Rxa5 40 Nc4 Rd5 41 Rf4 Nd7 42 Rxe6+ Kg5 43 g3 resigns.

#8. C.TORRE–SAEMISCH
Moscow, 1925

1 d4 Nf6 2 Nf3 e6 3 Bg5 c5 4 e3 Nc6

This is primarily a transpositional device.

5 Nbd2	b6
6 c3	Bb7
7 Bd3	cxd4
8 exd4	Be7
9 Nc4	

Torre liked the idea of overprotecting the e5 square, and employed this maneuver on a number of occasions.

9 0-0 0-0 10 Re1 is better for White, according to Balashov, who convincingly defeated Lebredo at Cienfuegos 1975 with it.

| 9 ... | Qc7 |

9...0-0 10 Qe2 Qc7 is similar, but in Janowski - Saemisch, Marianske Lazne 1925, White adopted a different, but equally effective plan: 11 h4!? h6 12 Qd2! Ng4 (12...hxg5 13 hxg5 Ne8 14 Bh7+ Kh8 15 Nce5 Nxe5 16 Nxe5 with the idea of Qf4 gives White a powerful attack. Note that 16...Bxg2 fails to 17 Be4+!) 13 Bf4! d6 14 Ne3! Nxe3 15 Qxe3 h5 16 Rh3 e5 17 dxe5 Nxe5 18

Nxe5 dxe5 19 Bxe5 Bd6

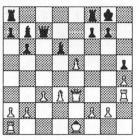

20 Qh6!! and Black resigned.

10 Qd2

10 Qe2! would have been more.

10 ...   Rc8

11 0-0

Black's formation looks solid, but he lacks counterplay and White is able to attack effectively.

11 ...   h6

12 Bf4   d6

13 Rfe1!

Seizing an important semi-open file, and keeping pressure on the center.

13 ...   Nd8

14 Qd1!

The queen has accomplished her task on one diagonal and now switches to d1-h5, in order to infiltrate the kingside.

14 ...   Nd5

15 Bg3   0-0

16 Nh4

This opens the diagonal for the queen.

16 ...   g5?

This is a critical weakening of the kingside which is punished in fine combinative fashion, exploiting the power of 13 Rfe1!

17 Qh5   Kg7
18 Rxe6!!   Nxe6

18...fxe6 19 Qg6+ Kh8 20 Qxh6+ Kg8 21 Qh7 mate.

19 Nf5+   Kg8
20 Nxh6+ resigns.

#9. SPASSKY–OSNOS
USSR Championship, 1963

1 d4 Nf6 2 Nf3 e6 3 Bg5 c5 4 e3 Qb6

This is a provacative move, and it leads to a complex variation which is at the heart of the theory of the Torre Attack.

5 Nbd2

The pawn sacrifice is much more promising than the cowardly 5 Qc1.

5...   Qxb2

a) 5...d5 6 Bxf6 gxf6 7 c4! cxd4 8 exd4 dxc4 9 Bxc4 Nc6 10 0-0 Bd7 11 d5! exd5 12 Qe2+ Ne7 13 Bxd5 0-0-0 14 Bxf7 Ng6 15 Nc4 Qa6 16 Rfd1 ± Spassky - A Zaitsev, USSR 1963.

b) 5...cxd4 6 Nxd4 Qxb2 7 Nb5 Na6 8 Rb1 Qe5 9 Bf4 Qc5 10 Nc4 Be7 (Alekseyev - Tolush, USSR 1962) 11 Nbd6+ Kf8 12 Rb5 Qc6 13 Be5 intending Na4 - Bellin (±).

6 Bd3

Black has eaten the poisoned pawn and now must choose between retreating the queen, acting in the center, or simply developing.

6 ...   cxd4

6...d5 and 6...Nc6 are considered in the next two games, but retreating the queen is not advisable:

a) 6...Qb6 7 0-0 cxd4 *(7...d6 8 dxc5 dxc5 9 e4 h6 10 Bh4 Nc6 11 Nc4 Qc7 12 Qb1! Nh5 13 Qb2! Be7 14 Bxe7 Qxe7 15 Nfe5! 0-0 16 Nxc6 bxc6 17 Qe5± Bondarevsky - Antoshin, Sochi 1964)* 8 exd4 Be7 9 Re1 Qc7 10 c4 b6 11 Rc1 d6 12 Bb1 Nbd7 13 Nf1 h6 14 Bh4 Bb7 15 Ne3± Nei - Mikenas, USSR Spartakiad 1967.

b) 6...Qc3 7 0-0 d5 8 Re1 c4 9 Bf1 Nc6 10 Bxf6 gxf6 11 e4! Kd8 12 Rb1 Bh6 13 exd5 exd5 14 Rb5! Bxd2 15 Rxd5+ Kc7 16 Nxd2 Be6 17 Ne4 Qb2 18 Rd6! f5 19 d5! fxe4 20 dxe6 fxe6 21 Rd7+ Kb6 22 Qd6 Rac8 23 Bxc4 Qxc2 24 Qa3! Rhf8 25 Qe3+ resigns, Alekseyev - Balashov, USSR 1972.

7 exd4   Qc3

7...Nc6 8 Rb1 and now:

a) 8...Qxa2 9 Bxf6 gxf6 10 Nc4 Qa4! *(10...Nb4 11 Ra1 Nxd3+ 12 cxd3 +- or 10...Bb4+ 11 Ke2 Bc3 12 Rb3 ±)* 11 0-0 Be7 12 Ne3 d5 (or else White advances to d5) 13 Bb5 Qa5 14 c4 with strong pressure;

b) 8...Qc3?! 9 Rb3 Qa5 10 0-0 Be7 11 Nc4 Qc7 12 Ne3 d5 13 c4! with compensation, for example 13...Na5 14 Rc3 Ne4 15 Bxe4 dxe4 16 Bxe7 exf3 17 Ba3! fxg2 18 Re1 Kd8 19 d5 Bd7 20 Bb4 Re8 21 c5! resigns, Larsen - Stern, U S Open 1970. The threat is 22 d6, and if 21...b6 then 22 c6 Bc8 23 d6.

8 0-0	d5
9 Re1	Be7

9...Nc6 is a possible alternative.

10 Re3	Qc7

11 Ne5!

Black's pieces are in no position to stop a kingside attack, and thus the king is locked in the center.

11 ...	Nc6

11...0-0? 12 Bxf6 Bxf6 13 Bxh7+!! Kxh7 14 Qh5+ Kg8 15 Rh3 +-.

12 c3	Nxe5
13 dxe5	Ng8

13...Ne4 14 Nxe4 dxe4 15 Bxe7 exd3 16 Bd6 Qxc3 17 Rxd3 Qa5 18 Rc1! (intending Bc7) 18...Bd7 19 Rc7 Qb5 20 Be7!

14 Nf3	h6
15 Bf4	Bd7
16 Nd4	Bg5
17 Bxg5	hxg5
18 Qg4	

White's command of the center and kingside pressure is overwhelming.

18 ...	Qxc3
19 Nb3	Nh6
20 Qxg5	Qb4
21 Rg3	Qf8?

A mistake, though Black is already in trouble, for example 21...g6 22 Qf6 Qf8 23 Nc5!

22 Rc1	f6

23 Qe3   f5
24 Nc5!

24 ...   f4

The fork is not important, but the opening of the diagonal is!

25 Bg6+   Ke7
26 Qa3!   resigns

#10. I.SOKOLOV–KI. GEORGIEV
Palma de Mallorca, 1989

1 d4 Nf6 2 Nf3 e6 3 Bg5 c5 4 e3 Qb6 5 Nbd2 Qxb2 6 Bd3 Nc6

7 0-0   d5

Black has to do something about the threat of 8 Nc4.

If 7...Qb6, then 8 Rb1 is strong, e.g., 8...Qd8 *(8...Qc7 9 Bxf6 gxf6 10 Ne4±)* 9 e4 cxd4 10 e5! h6 11 Bh4 g5 12 Bg3 Nd5 13 Ne4 with a crushing position for White, Knezevic - Stean, Cirella di Diamante 1976/77.

8 Bxf6   gxf6
9 c4!

By threatening to open up the center and expose the Black king, White places his opponent in a precarious position.

9 ...	Nb4
10 Be2	Qa3
11 e4!	

White is fully developed, while Black has but two pieces in the game. All that is needed now is an open line or two!

11 ...	dxe4
12 Nxe4	Be7
13 Qd2	Bd7

But not 13...0-0? 14 Qh6 ±.

14 Qf4	0-0-0

So the king has escaped, but the queenside is no safe haven!

15 Nxf6	cxd4
16 Nxd4	Bc6
17 Nb5!	Qa5
18 Ne4	Bxe4

18...f5 19 Ned6+ Bxd6 20 Nxd6+ Rxd6 21 Qxd6 and 21...Rg8 is not on because of 22 Qxe6+.

19 Qxf7	Rd7
20 Qxe6	Bc6

21 Bg4 h5 22 Bh3 Bd8 23 Rad1 Rhh7 24 a3 Nc2 25 Qg6! Rhe7 26 Qxc2 a6 27 Na7+ resigns

#11. SALOV–DE LA VILLA
Szirak Interzonal, 1987

1 d4 e6 2 Nf3 Nf6 3 Bg5 c5 4 e3 Qb6 5 Nbd2 Qxb2 6 Bd3 d5

This move has the advantage of taking charge of the center and threatening c4, but it allows a critical weakening of the kingside and White gets in c4 first.

7	Bxf6!	gxf6
8	c4!	Qc3
9	Be2	cxd4

9...dxc4 10 0-0 Qa5 11 Nxc4 Qc7 12 Rc1 Nc6 13 Ncd2 Be7 14 Ne4 and the knight maneuver brought White full compensation in Vaganian-Razuvayev, USSR Championship 1983.

10	Rc1	Qa5
11	cxd5	Na6

Forced, since 11...Bd7 12 dxe6 fxe6 13 Nxd4 Nc6 14 Bh5+ Ke7 15 0-0 is not much fun for Black.

12	Nxd4	Qxd5
13	0-0	

White has completed development and has a powerful light-squared bishop.

13	...	Be7
14	Bf3	Qd7

14...Qd8 15 Qb3 0-0 16 Bxb7 Rb8 17 Rxc8 ± - Salov.

15	Nc6!!	0-0

16 Qe2

White has more than sufficient compensation for a pawn, since Black's pieces are scattered ineffectively.

16 ...	Nb4
17 Nxb4	Bxb4
18 Ne4	Be7
19 Rfd1	

The domination of the open files combined with the weakness of the Black king make White's task an easy one.

19 ...	Qe8
20 Rc7	e5
21 Ng3	Bd8

21...Be6 22 Bxb7 Rd8 23 Bc6!

22 Rxc8!	Rxc8
23 Be4	f5

Or else Qg4+.

24 Nxf5	Kh8
25 Nd6	Qe6
26 Bf5	resigns

#12. DREYEV–LERNER
Simferopol, 1988

1 d4 Nf6 2 Nf3 e6 3 Bg5 c5 4 e3 h6!? 5 Bh4 b6 6 Nbd2 Be7 7 c3 0-0 8 Bd3

White has established a superior form of a Colle since his dark-squared bishop is deployed outside the pawn chain.

8 ...   Ba6

A reasonable plan, taking advantage of the fact that White has not castled and therefore must exchange light-squared bishops.

9 Bxa6   Nxa6
10 0-0   Nb8

The knight has no future on the queenside.

11 e4

White has achieved his strong center and therefore enjoys a small advantage.

11 ...   d5
12 dxc5   bxc5

12...dxe4? 13 Bxf6! and the Black pawn structure must suffer.

13 exd5   Qxd5
14 Qe2   Qb7

Or 14...Nc6 15 Nc4! followed by Rd1.

15 Ne5!?

A bold move, but then the Pb2 is poisoned.

15 ...   Nc6

15...Qxb2 16 Qf3 Na6 17 Nc6 Qb7 18 Nxe7+ Qxe7 19 Ne4 is much better for White since the pressure at f6 will cost Black more than a pawn.

16 Nd3   Nd7
17 Bg3   Na5
18 b3

Black now invests a pawn to disrupt the White queenside.

18 ...	c4
19 bxc4	Rfc8
20 Rab1	Qc6

20...Qa6 21 Nb4 Bxb4 22 cxb4 Nxc4 23 Rfc1 Ndb6 24 Rc2! intending Rbc1 (*24 a4? Qxa4! 25 Nxc4 Qb5!*) 24...Nxd2 25 Qxa6 Rxc2 26 Rd1 leaves Black without sufficient compensation for the queen.

21 Nb4	Qc5

21...Qa4 was perhaps better, though the queen would have been offside.

22 Rfd1	Nf6

22...Nb6?! 23 Na6 Qc6 24 c5 Bxc5 25 Nxc5 Qxc5 26 Rb5 Qxc3 27 Be5 Qa3 28 Qg4 would be most unpleasant for Black.

23 Na6	Qc6
24 c5	

Even without a light-squared bishop, the pawn will be able to advance with the help of the knights.

24 ...	Nd5

a) 24...Nb7 25 Nb4 Qxc5 26 Nd3 Qc6 27 Ne5 +−
b) 24...Rd8 25 Bc7!

25 Ne4	Qa4

26 Nb4

26 Rd4? would allow Black to turn the tables: 26...Nxc3! 27 Qd3 Qxd4! -+.

26 ...	Nf6!
27 Bd6	Nxe4
28 Qxe4	Bf6

The pawn at c3 is not relevant to the action, and White should have ignored it. Instead he chooses a plan that is appealing at first sight, but wrong.

29 Rd3?

The correct continuation was 29 f3! Bxc3 30 Nd5! (This is probably what White failed to find) 30...Qxe4 31 Ne7+ Kh7 32 fxe4 Rd8 33 c6 and Black is busted.

29 ...	Nc6
30 Qe2	Ne7
31 Qd1	Qxd1+
32 Rbxd1	a5
33 Nc2	

The endgame is still much better for White, since Black has no counterplay and no way of establishing a passed pawn on the kingside.

33 ...	Nf5
34 Na3!	

White finally realizes that the pawn at c3 is not important.

34 ...	Nxd6
35 cxd6	Rxc3
36 Rxc3	Bxc3
37 Nb5	

The occupation of this critical outpost gives White excellent winning chances, though the game is not beyond salvation yet for Black.

37 ...	Bf6
38 a4	Bd8
39 Rc1	Kf8
40 Kf1	Ke8
41 Rc7!	Kf8?!

a) 41...Ra6 42 Re7+ *(42 Ke2 Rb6 43 Ra7 Rc6 44 Kd3 Rc1=)* Kf8 43 Nc7 Bxc7 44 dxc7 Ra8 =.

b) 41...Rb8! 42 Rc4 and White retains a significant advantage, though Black may be able to hold with 42...Kd7.

42 Rb7!

42 Na7?! Rb8 43 Nc6 Bxc7.

| 42 ... | Rc8 |
| 43 Nc7 | |

Now we see the effects of the movement of the Black king to f8. The threat is simply that the White king can march up the diagonal and snare the Pa5.

43...	Bxc7
44 Rxc7	Rd8
45 Rc6	Ke8
46 Ra6	Kd7
47 Rxa5	Kxd6

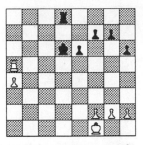

A well-known endgame formation. With careful play, Black can hold, and what follows demonstrates yet again the difficulty of playing rook endgames correctly even at grandmaster levels.

48 Ra7	Rf8?

Even strong players sometimes forget that in rook endgames, activity is the most important thing!

48...f5! 49 Rxg7 Ra8= 50 Rg6 Rxa4 51 Rxh6 is a known draw.

49 a5	Kc6
50 h4	g5
51 h5	g4
52 Ke2	f5
53 a6	Rb8
54 Rh7	

The difference between this position and the one before... Rf8 is that White has already advanced his h-pawn, the Black king is further offside, and the a- pawn is still on the board!

54...	Rb2+
55 Ke3	Ra2
56 Rxh6	Kd6?

56...Kd5! would have been more accurate.

57 Rg6!

57 Rh8 Rxa6 58 Kf4 Ra4+ 59 Kg5 g3! 60 f3 Ra2 61 h6 Rxg2 62 h7 Rh2 would only draw.

57 ...	Rxa6
58 h6	Ra1
59 Kf4	

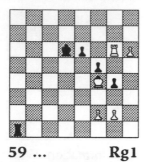

59 ...	Rg1

59...Rh1!? was a more resistant plan: 60 Kg5 Rh2 61 Rg7 Rxg2 62 h7 Rh2 63 Kg6 Ke5! Black can still hope for a draw after sacrificing the rook for the h-pawn, e.g., 64 Ra7 Kf4 65 Ra6 e5 66 Kg7 Rxh7+ 67 Kxh7 Kf3 68 Kg6 f4 69 Kf5 g3 70 fxg3 fxg3 71 Kxe5 g2 72 Rg6 Kf2 73 Rf6+ Ke1 =.

60 Rg8!

60 h7 Rh1 61 Rg7 Rh5.

60...	Rxg2
61 h7	Rxf2+
62 Kg3	Rf3+
63 Kg2	Rh3
64 h8Q	Rxh8
65 Rxh8	Ke5

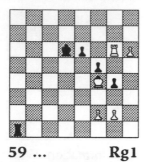

The difference between this and the other lines is the position of the White king, which is back home guarding the queening square instead of at h7 or h8.

66 Kg3	Ke4
67 Rh1	Ke5
68 Re1+	Kf6
69 Kf4	

The King plays an active role now that the enemy monarch has been driven back.

69...	Kf7
70 Ra1	Kf6

71 Ra6 Kf7 72 Ke5 Kg6 73 Rxe6+ Kg5 74 Re8 resigns

#13. THESING–HARTMANN
Bundesliga, 1986
1 Nf3 Nf6 2 d4 e6 3 Bg5 d5 4 e3 Nbd7

This is an attempt to transpose into standard Queen's Gambit lines after 5 c5, as was seen, for example, in Marshall - Bogoliubow, New York 1924.

5 Nbd2   Bd6
This move differentiates the line from the standard plans with Be7. If White manages to play e4, however, Black will have to worry about the fork at e5, so this idea entails a certain amount of risk.

6 Bd3   0-0
a) 6...h6 7 Bh4 c6 8 e4 That is possibly premature. 8...dxe4 9 Nxe4 Qa5+ 10 Qd2 Qxd2+ 11 Nfxd2 with a slight endgame advantage for White in Rivas - Rivera, Haifa Olympiad 1976.

b) 6...e5!? 7 e4 exd4 8 Nxd4 Ne5 and now:

b1) 9 exd5 is the consistent move: 9...Nxd3+ (9...Qe7 10 0-0 Nxd3 11 cxd3 Qe5 fails to 12 Re1) 10 cxd3 Qe7+ 11 Ne4 Bb4+ 12 Kf1 ±;

b2) 9 Be2 is wimpy: 9...Be7 10 exd5 Qxd5= Terrazas - Bedros, Siegen Olympiad 1970.

7 e4   e5

Black has achieved parity in the center, though White still has the initiative and the better placed bishop at g5.

8 exd5	Qe8
9 0-0	Nxd5
10 Re1!	

The game has taken on the nature of a 1 e4 e5 opening. By using man-on-man coverage (Re1 vs Qe8) White keeps his pressure on.

10 ...	f6
11 Bh4	Qh5
12 Bg3	

Now the Bg3 cuts through the diagonal and aims at the Bd6.

| 12 ... | Nf4 |
| 13 Nc4! | b5 |

A critical moment. After 14 Nxd6?! cxd6 Black would have an excellent game.

          14 dxe5!   Nxd3

Or 14...fxe5 15 Ncxe5 Nxe5 16 Nxe5 Qxd1 17 Raxd1 ±.

          15 Qxd3   Nc5

No better was 15...bxc4 16 Qd5+ Kh8 17 Qxa8 Nxe5 18 Nxe5 Bxe5 19 Bxe5 fxe5 20 Rad1 ±.

16 Qa3

There are lots of pieces hanging here, but the key factor, as throughout the early middlegame, has been the pressure at d6.

16 ...   fxe5

17 Nxd6 cxd6

18 Rad1

White has emerged with a clear positional advantage (2 pawn islands against 3) but he must activate his Bg3 and avoid a potential kingside attack.

18...	Bb7
19 Rxd6	Ne4
20 Rd7	Bc6
21 Qb3+!	Kh8
22 Rc7	Nxg3
23 Rxc6!	e4
24 hxg3	exf3
25 gxf3	Rxf3
26 Qe6!	

White's king is perfectly safe, and he now takes the initiative.

26 ...	Raf8
27 Re5	Rxg3+?

This sacrifice simply doesn't work, but Black was in deep trouble anyway, for example 27...Qf7 28 Qxf7 R3xf7 29 f4 Rb7 30 Kf2 h6 31 Ke3 ±.

28 fxg3	Qf3
29 Re2!	Qf1+
30 Kh2	Rf2+
31 Rxf2	Qxf2+

32 Kh3 Qf1+ 33 Kh4 Qh1+ 34 Kg5 Qc1+ 35 Kf5 Qf1+

36 Ke5 Qe1+ 37 Kd6 Qxg3+ 38 Kd7 h5 39 Qe8+ resigns.

#14. CAVENDISH–McLAREN
British Championship, 1990
1 Nf3 d5 2 d4 Nf6 3 Bg5 e6 4 e3 Be7 5 Nbd2 Ne4

This action is premature, even though it is one of the motivations of the line with an early Be7.

$$6\ Bxe7 \qquad Qxe7$$
$$7\ Bd3 \qquad Nxd2$$

a) 7...f5 8 Ne5 gives the White knight a secure outpost, while the Ne4 can be easily driven back with f2-f3: 8...0-0 9 0-0 Nxd2 10 Qxd2 Nd7 11 f4 Nxe5 *(11...Nf6 12 Rf3 Ne4 13 Bxe4 fxe4 14 Rg3 leaves Black with a permanently bad bishop, while White can use the outpost at e5 as a launching pad for a kingside attack)* 12 dxe5 Bd7 and despite the bad bishop, Black held on to draw in Petrosian - Lisitsyn, USSR Championship 1954.

b) 7...Nf6 8 0-0 0-0 9 Ne5 gives White too strong an initiative, e.g., 9... Nbd7 10 f4 Re8 11 Nxd7 Bxd7 12 Nf3 h6 13 Ne5 a6 14 Qd2 Rac8 15 g4 with an overpowering attack in Terrazas - Paris, Havana Olympiad 1966.

$$8\ Qxd2 \qquad Nd7$$
$$9\ e4!$$

White establishes a strong center and enjoys a better bishop as well, all at no cost in time since Black wasted moves with Ng8-f6-e4-d2.

         9 ...   dxe4

        10 Bxe4   c5

10...Nf6 11 Bd3 0-0 and White could castle in either direction with good attacking prospects and a lock on e5.

        11 0-0-0   Nf6

        12 Bd3   Bd7

        13 Qg5!

Interrupting Black's attempt to catch up in development.

        13 ...   Rc8

This is an invitation to open up the g-file, but White wisely declines.

        14 Ne5!

14 Qxg7 Rg8 15 Qh6 Rxg2 16 Bxh7 Rxf2 17 Ne5 cxd4 18 Rxd4 Nxh7 19 Qxh7 (*19 Rxd7 Qg5+ 20 Qxg5 Rcxc2+!* with the idea Nxg5 -+) 19...Rcxc2+ 20 Qxc2 Rxc2+ 21 Kxc2 Qc5+.

        14 ...   0-0

        15 Qh4   h6

White has deployed his forces and is prepared for the final assault with the advance of the g-pawn.

16	g4	Bc6
17	Rhg1	Nd5
18	g5	cxd4

Black must do something to open lines against the White king, since his own monarch has inadequate defense.

19	gxh6!	g6

19...Qxh4? 20 Rxg7+ Kh8 21 Rh7+ Kg8 22 Rg1+.

20	Rg5	Qf6

21	Nxg6!	fxg6
22	Rxg6+	Qxg6
23	Bxg6	Nf4
24	Qe7	resigns.

#15. KLINGER–GAST
Zurich, 1990

1 d4 Nf6 2 Nf3 e6 3 Bg5 Be7 4 Nbd2 b6

The Queen's Indian set up is a reasonable one, but in this move order White has an important resource.

5 e4!

Now play has tranposed into the Owen defense, a disreputable line for Black.

5 ...	Bb7
6 Bd3	d5
7 Qe2	

White is effectively a tempo up on the main lines, because he has achieved e2- e4 in one move instead of two.

7 ...	dxe4
8 Nxe4	0-0
9 Bxf6!	Bxf6
10 0-0-0	

White has a greater presence in the center, is better developed, and has a safe haven for his king on the queenside, allowing a rapid attack on the kingside.

10 ...	Nc6
11 c3	Ne7

This permits White to create a serious structural weakness in the Black camp, but the idea is to get the knight over to help with the kingside defense, and there was no other path.

12 Nxf6+	gxf6
13 Qd2!	Kg7

Otherwise the White queen will take up a powerful position at h6.

14 h4	Rg8
15 Rh3	Qf8?!

It might have been better to concede the pawn and let the king run away to the center. Now the Black position is cramped, and its forces cannot be used effectively.

16 Qf4!	

A clever move, gaining time to transfer to the kingside by sniping at the Pc7.

16 ...	Nd5

Or 16...c5? 17 Rg3+ Kh8 *(17...Ng6 18 h5 e5 19 h6+! Kh8 20 Qxf6+)* 18 Qxf6+ Rg7 19 dxc5 ±.

17 Qe4	Qd6
18 Rg3+	Kf8
19 Rxg8+	Kxg8

Now the h-pawn falls, and the game is brought to a rapid conclusion.

       20 Qxh7+   Kf8
       21 h5   Qf4+
       22 Rd2   Qg4

And now for a fine finish!

       23 Bg6!   fxg6
       24 hxg6   Ke8

25 Qf7+ Kd8 26 g7 Ne7 27 Qxf6 Bxf3 28 gxf3
and Black resigned, helpless in the face of Qf8+.

#16. KORCHNOI–KARPOV
Moscow (m/19), 1974
1 d4 Nf6 2 Bg5 e6 3 e4 h6 4 Bxf6 Qxf6 5 Nf3

We have now reached the position which can also arise via 1
d4 Nf6 2 Nf3 e6 3 Bg5 h6 4 Bxf6 Qxf6 5 e4.

            5 ...   d6

A sensible move which creates a "small center" formation. But
the drawback is clear - the dark squared bishop will find it difficult
to enter the game.

            6 Nc3!

In this particular formation the knight is better placed on c3
than on d2. For one thing, Black's best plan lies in fianchettoing his

Bf8, as we shall see, and with the Black queen at f6 and White knight at f3, c2-c3 is not needed.

6 ...   g6

There are quite a few alternatives:

a) 6...b6 is discussed in the context of 5...b6.

b) 6...a6 7 e5! Qd8 8 Bd3 d5 9 Ne2 c5 10 c3 (In this French position White benefits from the lead in development and lack of a problematic dark-squared bishop.) 10...Nc6 11 0-0 Bd7 12 Qd2 Qb6 (Tyerpugov - Botvinnik, USSR Championship 1951) 13 dxc5! Bxc5 14 b4 Be7 15 a4±.

c) 6...c6 7 e5! dxe5 8 dxe5 Qf4 9 g3 Qb4 10 a3 Qa5 (*10...Qxb2 11 Na4* traps the queen) 11 b4 Qc7 12 Ne4 and White has a significant initiative and spatial advantage. Petrosian - Taimanov, USSR Team Championship 1951 continued 12...a5 13 Rb1 axb4 14 axb4 Nd7 15 Nd6+! Bxd6 16 exd6 ±.

d) 6...g5 7 Bd3 Bg7 8 0-0 0-0 9 e5! Qe7 10 Qe2 d5 11 Nd1! c5 12 c3 Nc6 13 Ne3 Bd7 14 Rae1! cxd4 15 cxd4 gives White a position in which he can concentrate on attacking the enemy king with all of his forces, while Black lacks counterplay, Orso-Farago, Hungarian Championship 1979.

e) 6...Nd7 7 Qd2 g6 8 0-0-0 a6 9 h4 Bg7 transposes below.

7 Qd2!   Qe7

7...Bg7 is a more logical approach: 8 0-0-0 a6 9 h4 Nd7 10 g3 b5 11 e5! dxe5 12 Nxe5 Bb7 (*12...Nxe5 13 dxe5 Qxe5?? 14 Qd8+#*) 13 Nxd7 Kxd7 14 Rg1 unclear.

8 0-0-0   a6

Although White is way ahead in development, this move is necessary, because in order to catch up Black is going to have to create some concrete threats on the queenside.

9 h4   Bg7
10 g3   b5!

Korchnoi evaluates this position as unclear and much depends on the next few moves.

11 Bh3!

Korchnoi wisely realizes that the play is not going to take place on the long diagonal, but rather in the Black forecourt.

11 ...   b4

11...Nd7 might be wiser here, keeping the position closed. But complex play lies ahead, for example 12 e5!? (*12 d5?! e5* is unclear) 12...dxe5 (*12...Bb7 13 exd6 cxd6 14 d5 e5 leaves both Black bishops looking a little misplaced, and the Black king will have difficulty finding secure shelter. Both 15 g4 and 15 h5 are reasonable tries*) 13 d5 with a strong initiative which should compensate for the pawn.

12 Nd5!

Botvinnik indicates a clear advantage for White after this move, while the player of the White pieces was more modest, claiming only a slight advantage.

12 Ne2 a5 13 d5 is unclear, according to Botvinnik.

12 ...	exd5
13 Bxc8	0-0!
14 Bb7	Ra7
15 Bxd5	c6
16 Bb3	Qxe4

In this position White has two choices, and in the game Korchnoi went astray.

17 Qd3?!

17 Qf4! Qxf4+ 18 gxf4 would have led to a fracturing of the kingside pawn structure which would have been only temporary, since on the next move White would be able to advance one of the weak pawns with good attacking chances.

17 ...	Qxd3
18 Rxd3	Nd7

Black can now lay claim to full equality. The Bb3 is of little value.

19 Re1	Nb6
20 a4!	bxa3

Or else White will be able to redeploy the bishop at a4 after advancing the pawn further, for example 20...a5 21 c4 bxc3 22 bxc3 Rb8 23 Kc2 with the idea Rde3.

21 bxa3	a5
22 Rde3?!	

Premature. Better first 22 a4!

22 ...	Bf6?!

And here it is Black who should have taken advantage of White's error by 22...a4!

23 a4!

23 ...   c5?!

This seems to be a principled reaction to the central pawn formation, but it should have been better prepared. 23...Rc7! 24 Re4 d5! 25 R4e3 c5! was the proper sequence, since after 26 dxc5 Rxc5 Black keeps the Bb3 hemmed in and has significant queenside counterplay.

24 dxc5	dxc5
25 Nd2	Kg7
26 Rf3	Rc7
27 Nc4!	

This forces Black to enter an opposite-colored bishop ending where White has a small but annoying advantage.

27 ...	Nxc4
28 Bxc4	Rd8
29 c3	Rcd7
30 Kc2!	

White has a better game because his king is very active and will be able to take part in the queenside play. Yet Black should not lose, with careful play.

30 ...	Rd2+
31 Kb3	Rd1
32 Rxd1	Rxd1

33 Bb5!

This opens the path for the king.

33 ...   Rd5?!

It is understandable that Karpov felt his rook would be more actively placed in the middle of the board, but after 33...Rc1! 34 Kc4 Rc2! the pressure at c3 and f2 would have kept the game balanced.

34 Re3

34 Kc4! would have been much more efficient.

34 ...   Re5

35 Rd3

Obviously White would have no real winning chances in the pure bishop ending.

35 ...   Re2

36 Rf3   Re5?!

Karpov repeats the position, looking for a draw, but this gives Korchnoi a new chance to adopt the correct plan.

37 Kc4!   Rf5

38 Rd3

It is worth the pawn to avoid the bishop ending.

38...   Rxf2

39 Kxc5   Be5

40 Kb6   Rg2

41 c4   Rxg3

42 Rd7!

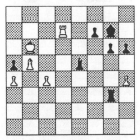

It is not the number of pawns that counts, it is how far away they are from the queening square!

42...   g5

43 hxg5   hxg5

44 c5	Rc3
45 c6	g4
46 c7	g3
47 Bc6!	

This wins the piece, but now it is Black who enjoys the advanced passed pawn.

47 ...	Bxc7+
48 Rxc7	

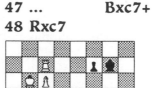

This is a critical position.

48 ...	Kh6?!

48...Rxc6+!! would have saved the game: 49 Rxc6 f5 (Connecting the passed pawns) 50 Rc1 Kf6 51 Rg1 (*51 Kxa5 f4 52 Rg1 Kf5 53 Kb4 Kg4 54 a5 f3 55 a6 f2 56 Ra1 g2 57 a7 g1Q 58 a8Q Qe1+! with a draw or 51 Kc5 Ke5=*) 51...f4 52 Kc5 Ke5 53 Re1+ Kf5 54 Kd4 Kg4! 55 Kd3 g2 56 Re8 Kg3 57 Rg8+ Kf2 58 Ke4 g1Q 59 Rxg1 Kxg1 60 Kxf4 Kf2 61 Ke4 Kg3 62 Kd5 Kf4 63 Kc5 Ke5 64 Kc6 Ke6 65 Kb5 Kd6 66 Kxa5 Kc7=.

49 Rc8	f5
50 Rf8	

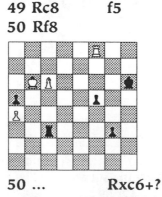

50 ...	Rxc6+?

There was one last chance available to Black, but it required seeing a very clever idea, and Karpov was not up to the task: 50

Rg8 f4 51 Ba8 f3 52 Kxa5 f2 53 Bg2 Rb3! 54 Ka6 Rb1 55 Rf8
Rg1 56 Bh3 Kg5 57 Kb7 Kh4 58 Rh8+ Kg5 59 a5 f1Q 60 Bxf1
Rxf1 61 a6 Kg4 (61...g2? 62 Rg8+) 62 a7 Ra1 63 a8Q Rxa8 64
Rxa8 g2 65 Ra1 Kf3=.

50...Kg5! was the right move, since it is important that the
Black king be as close as possible to the queening square. 51 Ba8
f4 52 Kxa5 Rb3! 53 Ka6 Kg4 54 a5 f3 55 Ka7 g2 56 Rg8+ Kh3
57 a6 Kh2 58 Rh8+ Kg3 59 Rg8+ Kf2 60 Bd5=.

51 Kxc6	Kg5
52 Rg8+!	Kf4
53 Kb5	Kf3
54 Kxa5	f4

54...g2 55 Kb4 Kf2 56 Kc3! g1Q 57 Rxg1 Kxg1 58 Kd3 Kh2
59 a5 f4 60 a6 f3 61 Ke3! Kg3 62 a7 f2 63 Ke2 Kg2 64 a8Q+ +-

55 Kb4	Kg2
56 a5	f3
57 a6	f2
58 a7	f1Q
59 a8Q+	Qf3
60 Qa2+	

60 Qxf3+?? Kxf3 61 Kc3 g2 62 Kd2 Kf2 63 Rf8+ Kg3 64
Rg8+ Kf2 =.

60...	Qf2
61 Qd5+	Qf3
62 Qd2+	Qf2
63 Kc3!	Kg1

63...Qxd2+ 64 Kxd2 Kf2 65 Rf8+ Kg1 66 Ke2 g2 67 Rg8
Kh1 68 Kf2+-.

64 Qd1+	Kg2
65 Qd3	Qc5+
66 Kb3	Qb6+
67 Kc2	Qc6+
68 Kd2	Qh6+
69 Qe3	Qh4
70 Rb8!	Qf6
71 Rb6	Qf5

72 Rb2	Kh2
73 Qh6+	Kg1
74 Qb6+	Kh2
75 Qb8	Kh3
76 Qh8+	Kg4
77 Rb4+	Kf3
78 Qh1+	Kf2

Or 78...g2 79 Rb3+.

| 79 Rb2 | resigns. |

17. KORCHNOI–KARPOV
Hastings, 1971/72

1 d4 Nf6 2 Nf3 e6 3 Bg5 b6 4 e4 h6 5 Bxf6 Qxf6

By transposition we have reached the position under discussion with 5...b6.

6 Bd3

This makes more sense than commiting the Nb1. 6 a3 was Korchnoi's choice against Keres, in the 33rd USSR Championship 1964/65 which saw 6...Bb7 7 Nc3 d6 8 Qd2 Nd7 9 0-0-0 g5 10 Nb5 but Keres could have continued 10...g4! 11 Nxc7+ Kd8∓.

| 6 ... | Bb7 |
| 7 Nbd2 | a6 |

a) 7...c5 8 e5 Qd8 9 Be4 Qc7 10 0-0 Be7 11 Re1 0-0 12 dxc5 bxc5 13 Bxb7 Qxb7 14 Nc4 ± Levenfish - Rabinovich, Petrograd 1921.

b) 7...d6 is considered the best move for Black, but even so it is hard to achieve an equal game: 8 Qe2 g5 (8...Qd8 9 h4! a6 10 0-0-0 Nd7 11 g4 g6 12 c3 Bg7 13 Kb1 White stands better, thanks to his control of the center and secure king, as in *Kjarner-Ornstein*,

Tallinn 1977 or *8...g6 9 h4 Bg7 10 c3 Qe7 11 0-0-0 Nd7 12 Kb1 0-0-0 13 Ba6 c6 14 Ne1 Rhe8 15 Nc2 Nb8 16 Bxb7+ Kxb7 17 h5 g5 18 Rhe1± Speelman - Blackstock, China 1981)* 9 e5 Qe7 10 0-0-0 is an improvement on the illogical kingside castling strategy employed in the game Rastianis-Kaunas, USSR 1978.

c) 7...Nc6 8 c3 0-0-0 9 Qe2 Kb8 10 Ba6 Ba8 11 a4! with a strong attack.

8 Qe2	d6
9 0-0-0	Nd7
10 Kb1	e5?!

Premature action in the center is generally unwise. 10...Qd8 would have allowed Black to regroup with Be7 and kingside castling.

11 c3	Be7

Now the Qf6 is awkwardly placed, although 11...g6 12 h4 Bg7 13 g4 gives White a dangerous initiative.

12 Nc4	0-0
13 Bc2	Rfe8

13...exd4 14 cxd4 Rfe8 15 e5! ±.

14 d5!

This is a principled decision, closing the center and limiting the power of the Bb7. With the exception of the queenside castling, the structure bears a relationship to that of a Spanish.

14 ...	c5?

a) 14...c6! would have been more in the spirit of the variation, e.g., 15 Ne3 b5 16 g4!? with an unclear position in which White's kingside play seems more promising to me.

b) 14...Bf8 is another Spanish maneuver which comes into consideration here, followed by c7-c6.

15 Ne3	Bf8

16 g4!   Qd8
17 g5!

White wastes no time.

17 ...   h5

a)17...hxg5 18 Rdg1 and the Black king is a dead duck.

b)17...g6 18 gxh6 Bxh6 19 h4 Bf4 is perhaps the best defense, though the king will still be vulnerable.

18 g6!

White just keeps on coming!

18 ...   fxg6
19 Rhg1   Qf6
20 Ng5   Be7
21 Ne6   Nf8

A logical plan, showing proper respect for the attack.

21...Rac8 22 Rg2 Nf8 23 Rdg1! Kh7 24 Nxf8+ Rxf8 25 Rxg6! Qxg6 26 Rxg6 Kxg6 27 Nf5 ±.

22 Nc7   Qf7
23 Rdf1?!

Taking the exchange is hardly worth anything but with 23 a4 and then Bc2-d3 White would hve been able to create crushing pressure on the queenside. Instead Korchnoi winds up merely gaining a minor material advantage.

23 ...   b5!
24 Nxa8   Bxa8

Considering thatBlack's counterplay lies on the queenside, the capture with the rook would have been far more sensible.

25 c4   Rb8
26 Bd3

26 ...   Qe8

26...b4 might have been the best try, though after 27 Bc2! White would reposition his bishop on the light squares, and the impotent Ba8 would be yet another problem for Black. For example 27...Bb7 28 f4 exf4 29 Ng2 g5 *(29...Bg5 30 e5 dxe5 31 Qxe5 ±)* 30 e5 dxe5 31 Qxe5 Rd8 32 Nxf4!! gxf4 33 Rxf4 +-.

27 Rc1   Bf6
28 Rg2   Rb6?!

Karpov tries to correct his previous error by transferring his bishop to c8 via b7, but again 28...b4 was probably the best try.

29 Rcg1!

This exploits the new weakness of the back rank. In addition, it creates the threat of capturing at g6 and then at h5.

29 ...   Rb8

Admitting the error.

30 Qf1!   b4

30...Bb7 31 cxb5! Bc8 32 bxa6 Bh3 33 Qc2 Bxg2 34 Rxg2 and the queenside pawns are decisive.

31 Be2   h4

32 Rxg6!!   Qxg6

32...Nxg6 33 Bh5.

33 Rxg6   Nxg6

34 Bg4	Nf4
35 Qd1!	b3

35...Bb7 36 Qa4 Rd8 37 Nf5 ±.

36 axb3	Bb7
37 Ng2	Bc8

37...Nxg2 allows terminal infiltration: 38 Be6+ Kf8 39 Qh5.

38 Bxc8	Rxc8
39 Qg4	Re8

40 Nxf4 exf4 41 Qxf4 Be5 42 Qxh4 Rf8 43 b4 Bd4
44 bxc5

and Black resigned since the time control had passed and the pawns soon will.

#18. MURSHED–CONQUEST
London (Nat West), 1989
1 d4 Nf6 2 Nf3 e6 3 Bg5 h6 4 Bxf6 Qxf6 5 e4 b6

More common is 5...d6, but this move is also playable. White is permitted to advance his e-pawn, but the a8-h1 diagonal will be dominated by Bb7.

6 Bd3	Bb7
7 Nc3	g5!?

A provocative and rather risky plan.

a) 7...d6 8 0-0 Nd7 is considered equal by Keres, though after 9 Qe2 White's superior development should count for something.

b) 7...Bb4 8 0-0 Bxc3 9 bxc3 0-0 10 Nd2! d6 11 f4 Nd7 12 e5 Qe7 gave White a better game in Nei - Rytov, Tallinn 1973. 13 Qe2 followed by Rae1 would have been the most principled continuation.

8 Qe2	Nc6

| 9 e5 | Qg7 |
| 10 Ne4 | |

The position looks quite good for White, who dominates the center and can take advantage of the hole at f6. But d4 is very weak.

10 ...	g4
11 Nf6+!?	Kd8
12 Nd2	Nxd4
13 Qe3	Bc5
14 Qg3	

This is all pretty much forced, and Black has a pawn and good development, in return for which he had to give up on castling. Now he attacks the outpost f6.

14 ...	Be7
15 Qf4	Nc6
16 Nde4	

White has secured his outpost and has full compensation for his pawn. Black's king must still seek safety, and the kingside pawns are still weak.

| 16 ... | Kc8 |
| 17 0-0-0 | Bxf6 |

	18 Nxf6	Qg5

When one is a pawn up it makes sense to trade queens, but in this case there is an extra motivation - the White queen is effective on the dark squares and should be removed.

19	Qxg5	hxg5
20	Nxg4	Nb4

Black has returned the pawn, but now creates threats in the endgame. White has a number of weaknesses, at a2, e5, and g2. But without the participation of the Ra8, Black cannot compete, and must soon lose valuable time.

21	f3	Nxa2+
22	Kb1	Nb4
23	Bb5!	Bc6
24	Bxc6	dxc6

24...Nxc6 25 g3 a5 is the only way to get the Ra8 into the game without sacrificing the Pd7, but 26 h4 gxh4 27 gxh4 a4 28 h5 Ra5 29 f4 is still ± .

25	Rd2	c5
26	c3	Nc6
27	g3	

White prepares f3-f4, after which the Pe5 will be defended so that the Ng4 is free for other tasks. Notice that Black still has problems activating his rook, a consequence of his opening strategy.

27	...	Kb7
28	h4	gxh4
29	Rxh4	Rad8
30	Kc2	Rxd2+
31	Kxd2	Rd8+

31...Rxh4 32 gxh4 Ne7 33 h5 +-.

32	Ke2	c4
33	Rh7	Rd5
34	f4	Rb5

From here on, play becomes increasingly desperate for Black, who places all of his hopes on the a-pawn.

35	Rxf7	Rxb2+
36	Kd1!	

It is important for the king to remain as close to a1 as possible.

36 ...	a5
37 Ne3	b5
38 g4	Rf2
39 Rf6	

39 f5 Nxe5 40 Rf6 Nd3 41 Rxe6 Nb2+ 42 Kc1 Nd3+ 43 Kb1 Rb2+ 44 Ka1 Rb3 45 f6 Ra3+ 46 Kb1 Rb3+ 47 Kc2 a4 48 f7 a3 49 f8Q a2 50 Qf3+ Ka7 51 Re8 Rb2+ 52 Kd1 a1Q+ would have been one possible conclusion.

39 ...	a4
40 Nc2	Na5

In this continuation, the Black knight will take up a less useful post at b3.

41 f5	exf5
42 e6	Rf1+
43 Kd2	Nb3+
44 Ke3	Kc6
45 gxf5	

The two connected passed pawns should be decisive, but there are some wrinkles yet.

45 ...	Nc5
46 Nd4+	

46 e7+ Kd7 47 Rf7 Ke8!

46...	Kd6
47 Nxb5+	Ke5
48 Rf7	Re1+
49 Kd2	Re4
50 e7	Kf4
51 Nxc7	a3
52 Ne6+	

Or 52 e8Q Rxe8 53 Nxe8 a2 54 Ra7 Nb3+ 55 Kd1 *(55 Ke2? Kxf5! 56 Rxa2 Nc1+)* a1Q+ 56 Rxa1 Nxa1 57 f6 +-.

52...Kg3	53
e8Q	Nb3+
54 Kd1	Kf2
55 Ng7!	a2

55...Rxe8 56 Nxe8 a2 57 Ra7 a1Q+ 58 Rxa1 Nxa1 59 f6.

56 Ra7   resigns

CHAPTER TWO
1 d4 Nf6 2 Nf3 g6 3 Bg5

The King's Indian formation is considered the best reply to the Torre Attack, but White still obtains excellent prospects based on his sound opening strategy.

19. SPASSKY–BEREZHNOY
Kharkov, 1963

1 d4 Nf6 2 Nf3 g6 3 Bg5 Ne4

An approach which is similar to that of the Trompowski, which, however, is not generally considered fertile ground for the g6 plan.

4 Bh4   d5

4...c5 5 c3 Bg7 *(5...Qb6 6 Nbd2! Nxd2 7 Qxd2 cxd4 8 Nxd4* was slightly better for White in *Trifunovic - Pirc, Yugoslav Championship 1952* because White had a lead in development and controlled more space.) 6 Nbd2 Nxd2 7 Qxd2 cxd4 8 Nxd4 gives White a spatial advantage. Here, instead of 8...0-0 (Bellon - Fraguela, Lanzarote 1975) Black should play 8...d5, in order to prevent 9 e4.

5 e3   Bg7

5...b6 6 Ne5! c6 7 f3 Nd6 8 Nd2 Bg7 9 Bd3 +=, Vlansky - Neyelov, correspondence 1966.

6 Nbd2   c5

Black must take some action in the center, or fall behind in development, for example 6...Nd6 7 c3 c6 8 Be2 Nd7 9 0-0 Nf5 10 Bg5 f6 11 Bf4 g5 12 Bd3! e6 13 Bxf5 exf5 14 Bd6 Nf8 15 Ba3! gave White a clear advantage in Petrosian - Furman, USSR Championship 1958.

7 c3

                7 ...   cxd4

7...Nxd2 8 Qxd2 b6 9 Ne5! 0-0 10 f4 Bb7 11 Bd3 Nd7 12 0-0 gave White a most favorable version of the Colle attack in Gereben - Trincardi, Reggio Emilia 1963/64.

                8 exd4   0-0

8...Nc6 9 Nxe4! dxe4 10 Ng5 Bf6 11 d5! gave White a great game in Filip - Molnar, Lyons 1955.

                9 Nxe4   dxe4
                10 Nd2   f5
                11 Bc4+   Kh8
                12 Bg5

The White bishops are tearing the Black position apart.

                12 ...   Qe8
                13 h4   e5

This counters the flank operation with a central thrust, as recommended on general principles, but it is still too slow, and the White attack plays itself. 13...h6 would be met strongly by 14 h4!

                14 dxe5

Necessary, or else Black will play 14...exd4 followed 15...e3.

                14 ...   Nc6
                15 h5!   Nxe5
                16 hxg6   Qxg6
                17 Qh5!

White will not need his queen to complete this task!

                17 ...   Qxh5
                18 Rxh5   Nxc4
                19 Nxc4   Be6

Black has the bishop pair, but the kingside is still weak and now White aims for the center.

	20 Nd6!	Be5	21 0-0-0!
	Rg8		

21...Bxd5 22 Rxd6 Rae8 23 b3 and Black has nothing useful.

	22 g3	Rg7
	23 Be3	

Not only is the Pf5 threatened, but Bd4 is coming too.

	23...	Bxd6
	24 Rxd6	

Despite the opposite colored bishops, Black is busted.

	24...	Rg6
	25 b3	Kg8
	26 Bd4	Re8
	27 Rh1!	

The rook has done its job on the h-file, and can safely return home.

	27...	a6
	28 Kd2!	

Spassky is well-known for his aggressive king!

28... Rf8
29 Ke3 h6 30 Be5 Rc8 31 Rhd1 Rc5 32 Kd4! Rc8 33 c4 Bf7 34 Ke3! Be6 35 Rb6 Bf7 36 Rxb7 Be8 37 Ra7 h5 38 Rd5! 1-0

This final central occupation forced Black's resignation, as the rook will be effective along the 5th rank.

#20. KASPAROV–MARTINOVIC
Baku, 1980

1 d4 Nf6 2 Nf3 g6 3 Bg5 Bg7 4 Nbd2 d6 5 e4 0-0 6 c3 Nbd7 7 Be2

7 ...   **e5**

This move is very much in the spirit of the King's Indian Defense. Black takes aim at the White center. If White is not careful, a timely exd4 will leave the Pe4 weak, while the advance d4-d5 will allow Black counterplay with f7-f5. 7...h6 8 Bh4 g5 9 Bg3 Nh5. (Black is playing with great aggression, but his kingside will be weak.) 10 Nc4!? (An interesting idea, but White fails to follow it up correctly.) 10...e6 11 Nfd2 (Forcing matters, but *11 Ne3* was a more solid approach.) 11...Nf4 12 0-0 b6! (Suddenly the long diagonal is a promising target for the Bc8.) 13 Bf3 Bb7 14 Re1 Qe7 15 a4 a5 16 Nf1 Ba6! Black's bishop finds another useful post, and already it seems that his game is to be preferred, Seret - Nunn, Marbella Zonal 1982.

8 dxe5   **dxe5**
9 0-0   **b6**

9...c6 leaves the d6-square too weak: 10 Nc4 Qe7 11 Nd6≠.

10 Re1   **Bb7**
11 Qc2   **h6**

Black must do something to take the pressure off the pin.

12 Bh4   **Qe7**
13 Bf1   **Rfe8?!**

Both sides have just about completed development and it is time to make a plan for the middlegame. 13...Rfd8 was the correct move, because the e-file is not going to be the location of any important activity. By misplacing his rook, Black conceded a valuable tempo to be forfeited at a later time. With Black overprotecting the e-file, Kasparov shifts to the queenside.

14 b4!

This move gains important space on the queenside. Fooling around with the knights would have been less effective: 14 Nc4 Qe6 15 Nfd2 Qg4! 16 Bg3 *(16 Bxf6 Nxf6=)* Nh5 17 f3 Qg5 18 Bf2 Nf4 19 Kh1 h5 with a formidable attack for Black.

14 ...   a6

14...a5 would have challenged White's expansionist plans, but after 15 a3 Ra7 16 Bd3 Rea8 the tempo lost with Rf8-e8 proves to be important, as white has time for 17 Qb2! after which he holds a small but significant advantage.

15 Nc4

15...   Rac8?

A mistake in a difficult position.

a) 15...c5 16 Rad1 cxb4 17 Nd6 Reb8 18 Bc4! and the pressure is unbearable.

b) 15...Qe6! breaks the pin with tempo and then 16 Nfd2 c5 17 Ne3 cxb4 18 cxb4 Rac8 19 Qb1 gives White a smaller, but still significant advantage. The battle will take place on the light squares, which White will occupy with Bc4, since 19...a5 is met by 20 a4!.

16 a4!

Securing even more space on the queenside.

16 ...	Qe6
17 Nfd2	Nh5
18 f3	

Now White's dark-squared bishop will be a full-fledged member of the army, controlling important dark-squares along the g1-a7 diagonal.

18 ...	Bf6?!

Because White is going to retreat the bishop anyway, this simply blocks a useful retreat square for the knight.

19 Bf2	Bg5

More time-wasting. The bishop should have stayed at g7, where it could get to f8 more easily.

20 Ne3	Ndf6

Black becomes more and more entangled in his own web.

21 c4!	c6
22 Nb3	Nd7

22...Bxe3? fails to 23 Bxe3 hitting pawns at h6 and b6.

23 c5	b5
24 Red1	

Now we see why the bishop should have stayed home. The d6-square is now too vulnerable.

24 ...	Be7

Observing that the Black queen has no place to run, Kasparov unleashes a shot!

25 Nc4!	Rc7

25...bxc4? 26 Bxc4 Qf6 27 Rxd7 Rb8 28 Na5 Bc8 29 Rc7 Rxb4 30 Nxc6! Rb7 31 Nxe7+ +-.

26 Nd6	Rb8

27 axb5	cxb5
28 Nxb7	Rbxb7
29 Qa2!	Nb8
30 Na5	Qxa2
31 Rxa2	Ra7

31...Rd7 loses to 32 Rd5.

32 c6	Ra8
33 Rc2!	Bxb4

34 Rd8+ Kg7 35 Bb6 Bxa5 36 Bxa5 Rxc6 37 Rxb8 Rxb8 38 Rxc6 b4 39 Bc7 resigns.

[Notes after Kasparov]

#21. GANT–BOLANOS
Novi Sad Olympiad, 1990

1 d4 Nf6 2 Nf3 g6 3 Bg5 Bg7 4 Nbd2 0-0 5 c3 d6 6 e4 c5 7 dxc5 dxc5 8 Be2 Nc6 9 0-0 h6 10 Bf4 Nh5 11 Be3 b6 12 Qc2 e5 13 Rad1

13...	Qe7
14 Bb5	Bb7
15 Nc4	Rad8?!

White has a slight advantage in that Black's pawn structure limits the scope of the Bg7. By liquidating the major artillery, Black accepts an endgame in which he stands slightly worse.

16 Rxd8	Rxd8
17 Rd1	Nb8
18 Rxd8+	Qxd8
19 Qd2	Qxd2
20 Nfxd2	

20 ...	a6?

A misguided plan that leads to an inferior endgame.

21 Ba4	b5
22 Na5!	Ba8
23 Bd1	Nf6

Or else Bxh5 would have shattered the Black pawn structure, for which the pair of bishops, blockaded by friendly and enemy pawns, would have been no compensation.

24 Bxc5	Nxe4
25 Nxe4	Bxe4
26 a4	Nd7
27 Be3	Bd3
28 Nc6	e4?

29 Nb4	Ne5

29...bxa4 30 Nxd3 exd3 31 Bxa4 and the bishop pair combined with the vulnerability of the Pd3 gives White all the winning chances.

30 Nxa6	bxa4
31 Nc5	a3
32 bxa3	Nc4
33 Bc1	Bxc3

34	a4	g5
35	Bb3	Nb6
36	Be3	

Threatening 37. Nxd3!

36...		Nc8
37	f3	Nd6

38 fxe4 Bxe4 39 Nxe4 Nxe4 40 Bb6 Nd2 41 Bd5 Kf8 42 a5 resigns.

#22. VOGT–HAZAI
Leipzig, 1986

1 Nf3 Nf6 2 d4 g6 3 Bg5 Bg7 4 Nbd2 d6 5 e4 0-0 6 c3 Nc6 7 Bb5

Developing with tempo keeps the initiative in White's hands.

7 ...	Bd7

7...a6 8 Ba4 Bd7 9 0-0 h6 10 Bh4 leaves Black without an effective plan: 10...Qe8 (*10...b5 11 Bc2 e5 12 dxe5 dxe5 13 Re1 Be6 14 Bb3! Qe7 15 Bd5! Qd7 16 Bxc6 Qxc6 17 Nxe5 ± Sahovic - Lehmann, Wijk ann Zee 1972.*) 11 e5! Nh5 12 Re1 d5 13 Bc2 Nd8 14 Nf1 Ne6 15 Ne3 c6 16 Bg3 Nxg3 17 hxg3 Qd8 18 Nh4 Qb6 19 Rb1! Ng5 20 f4 Ne4 21 Bxe4 dxe4 22 Qc2 ± Darga - Ciocaltea, Siegen 1970.

8 0-0	Qe8
9 a4	a6
10 Be2	e5
11 d5	Ne7

The game has now reached a position similar to a King's Indian, save that the pawn is still at c3.

12 Qb3	Bc8

13 Ne1	Nd7
14 Nd3	f5
15 Qc4!	Nf6

This concedes the Pc7, but there wasn't much choice: 15...Qd8 16 Bxe7 Qxe7 17 Qxc7.

16 Bxf6	Rxf6
17 Qxc7	Bh6
18 f4	exf4
19 Nxf4	Bd7
20 Qxb7	Rb8
21 Qxa6	

These pawns aren't poisoned!

21 ...	Qf8

Playing for tricks.

22 Nc4	fxe4

23 Ne6! Bxe6 24 Rxf6 Qxf6 25 Qxd6 resigns

#23. SALOV–ROMANISHIN
Leningrad, 1987

1 d4 Nf6 2 Nf3 g6 3 Bg5 Bg7 4 Nbd2 0-0 5 c3 d6 6 e4 Qe8

An interesting new plan from the creative theoretician. The e5 square is supported directly, and when the Pe7 advances, there will not be a pin at f6.

7 Be2	Nc6

An additional point of this move order is that the development of the knight at c6 waits until after White has committed the Bf1, so that now Bb5 would entail a waste of a tempo.

8 0-0	e5

>9 dxe5   dxe5
>10 Qc2

The position resembles a Pirc, but the fact that White controls d4 is of considerable importance.

>10 ...   Nd8

Black wants to redeploy the piece with Ne6.

>11 Bh4   Nh5
>12 Rfe1   Ne6
>13 Nc4   Nef4
>14 Bf1

Play has proceeded logically. Black is attempting to attack on the kingside, while White adopts a defensive posture there and eyes the queenside.

>14 ...   Bg4
>15 Nfd2

White cannot allow Bxf3, of course.

>15 ...   Be6
>16 b4   Bxc4
>17 Nxc4   Bf6
>18 Bxf6   Nxf6

This position seems equal, at first glance, but the pressure at e5 renders Black's position a bit shaky.

>19 g3   N4h5

19...Ne6? 20 Nxe5 Nc5 21 Nxg6 hxg6 22 bxc5 ± .

>20 Rad1

White finally seizes the open file, and is now ready to play on the queenside.

>20 ...   b6
>21 a4   Qe6

22 a5	Rfe8

Black's defensive strategy involves overprotecting the Pe5. The Nh5 will be able to re-enter the game via g7 and e6 - if White gives it time.

23 Qa4	Ng7
24 Rd2	h6

The idea behind this move is to make a home for the Nf6 at h7, from which it may be able to take up an attacking post at g5.

25 Qd1	Qc6
26 Qf3	Qe6
27 Red1	

White's advantage is now obvious - he dominates the d-file, and the bishop will be more powerful than the knight in the endgame.

27 ...	g5
28 a6!	

This creates long-term problems for Black in any endgame, since the Pa7 will have to be guarded.

28 ...	g4
29 Qe3	Nh7
30 Rd7	Ng5

Black's attack is hardly to be feared, given that it is a lone horse against a well-defended king.

31 Rxc7	Red8
32 Rxd8+	Rxd8
33 Be2!	

Black's rook has taken over the d-file, but without access to any square along it the rook will not be able to have any real effect. In the meantime, the Pa7 is looking very weak.

33 ...		Nf3+
34 Kg2		b5
35 Na5		Ne1+
36 Kf1		Qa2

A clever resource, but one which is not sufficient.

37 Bxg4!

Not 37 Kxe1?? Qb1+.

37 ...		Nd3
38 Nc6		Rd6
39 Ne7+!		Kf8
40 Nd5		

With the d-file now closed, the White king is completely safe and the Black king is the one that must worry, with its defenders scattered to the wind.

40 ...		Qb1+
41 Kg2		Ne8

Black resigned this presumably adjourned position, because after 42 Qxa7 his game is hopeless. Resigns.

#24. SMYSLOV–NUNN
Tilburg, 1982

1 d4 Nf6 2 Nf3 g6 3 Bg5 Bg7 4 Nbd2 0-0 5 e4 d6 6 c3 h6 7 Bh4

Does driving the bishop back have any effect in this formation? Yes - it does further weaken the kingside fortress.

7 ...		Nc6
8 Bb5		Bd7
9 0-0		a6
10 Bc4		

Here is where the play differs from the 6...Nc6 line. The bishop retreats not to a4, as is more common there, but to c4.

10 ...	e5
11 dxe5	dxe5
12 Re1!	

Overprotection of e4 frees up the minor pieces for more useful tasks.

| 12 ... | Qe8 |

12...b5 13 Bf1 followed by an eventual a2-a4 would put strong pressure on the queenside.

13 a4	Nh5
14 Nb3	g5
15 Bg3	Rd8
16 Nfd2	

White's pieces have been quckly transferred to the queenside. Black's pieces, especially the offside knight, cannot get there so quickly.

16...	Nxg3
17 hxg3	Kh8
18 Qe2	Qe7
19 Nf1!	

The exchange of the Black knight for the Bg3 has created new opportunities on the kingside. Smyslov is the master of harmonic play - his pieces are often ready to switch to new targets quickly.

19...	Qf6
20 Nc5	Bc8
21 Ne3	Ne7
22 a5	Qg6

Black has chosen to sue the Bc8 to defend the queenside, but the heavy guns are all on the kingside, and White controls a bit more of the center. But before foraging on the queenside, Smyslov squashes the counterplay.

23 g4!	b6?!	

Black is paralyzed on the kingside, unable to transfer the knight to f4 due to the placement of the queen at g6. But this sacrifice of a queenside pawn leads to disaster.

24 Nf5!   Nxf5

24...bxc5 25 Nxe7 Qd6 26 Nxc8 Rxc8 27 Bxa6 ±.

25 gxf5   Qc6
26 Nxa6   Bxa6
27 Bxa6   bxa5
28 Rxa5

Now White has an extra pawn and better bishop The rest is easy for a player of Smyslov's caliber.

28...   Ra8

29 Rea1 Rfd8 30 Bc4 Rxa5 31 Rxa5 Kg8 32 Ra6 Qd7 33 Bd5 Qe7 34 Qh5 Rd6 35 Rxd6 cxd6 36 b4 resigns

#25. FELLER–OKOTH
Novi Sad Olympiad, 1990

1 d4 Nf6 2 Nf3 g6 3 Bg5 Bg7 4 Nbd2 d6 5 e4 0-0 6 c3 b6 7 Bc4 h6

Or 7...Bb7 8 Qe2 c5 9 dxc5 dxc5 10 0-0 Nc6 11 Ba6! Qb8 12 Bxb7 Qxb7 13 Nc4 Nd7 14 Rfe1 Rab8 15 Rac1 Qa6 16 b3 Qb7 17 h4 with a good attack for White, Szily - Liptay, Hungary Championship 1965.

8 Bh4   Bb7
9 Qe2

Black's double fianchetto plan is not effective against White's coordinated pieces.

9 ...	a5
10 0-0-0!?	

Castling kingside would have been safer, but Black's pieces cannot act well on the queenside.

10 ...	d5
11 exd5	Bxd5
12 Rhe1	Re8
13 Ne5	

White effectively dominates the center.

13 ...	c6
14 Kb1	Bxc4
15 Ndxc4	b5

Black makes a stab at gaining the initiative, but he is in for an unpleasant surprise.

16 Nxf7!!	Qd7

a) 16...Kxf7 17 Qe6+ Kf8 18 Ne5 and mate follows.

b) 16...bxc4 17 Nxd8.

17 Bxf6	bxc4

17...Bxf6 (17...Kxf7+ 18 Ne5+!) 18 Nxh6+ Kh7 (18...Kg7 19 Ne5 Bxe5 20 Qxe5+ Kxh6 21 Re3!) 19 Ne5! Bxe5 20 Qxe5 Kxh6 21 Re3!.

18 Bxg7	Qf5+

Black was in deep trouble in any event, e.g., 18...Kxg7 19 Ne5 ± or 18...Kxf7 19 Bxh6 ±. Now the rest requires no commentary.

19 Qe4	Kxf7

20 Bxh6 Nd7 21 Qxf5+ gxf5 22 Bg5 ± e6 23 h4 Nb6 24 g3 Nd5 25 g4 a4 26 a3 Rab8 27 Kc2 Rb7 28 gxf5

exf5 29 Rxe8 Kxe8 30 Re1+ Kd7 31 h5 Kd6 32 h6
Rh7 33 Re8 f4 34 Kc1 c5 35 Rd8+ Ke6 36 dxc5 Ke5
37 c6 Nc7 38 Rd7 resigns

#26. LANGEWEG–THIEL
Lugano, 1989

1 d4 Nf6 2 Nf3 g6 3 Bg5 Bg7 4 Nbd2 0-0 5 e4 d6 6
c3 c6

This formation, common recently in the Pirc defense, is not
likely to achieve equality.

7 Be2	Qc7
8 0-0	e5
9 dxe5	dxe5
10 h3	Nbd7
11 Qc2	Nc5
12 Be3	Ne6

Both sides develop in conformity with the principles of the
opening. The pawn structures are fairly similar, but White has
much more scope for the bishops and cleaner development for the
rooks, so he has better chances here.

13 Rfd1	Nh5
14 a4	Nef4
15 Bf1	

The motifs are similar to those of the Smyslov - Nunn game.

15...	Qe7
16 b4	Ne6
17 Nc4	f5

Black is playing actively for a kingside attack, but White is
making solid progress on the queenside and his king is well-

defended. That is probably why Black was willing to invest a pawn to speed up the attack.

18	Ncxe5	Bxe5
19	Nxe5	f4
20	Bd4	f3
21	g3	Ng5
22	Kh2	

In return for the pawn Black has put an end to queenside play. He has a strong point at f3 and the Bc8 can now enter the battle.

22...	Be6
23 h4!	

This further weakens the kingside, but gains the Pf3.

23...	Nf7
24 Nxf3	Qc7
25 e5 ±	Bg4
26 Bg2	Bxf3
27 Bxf3	Nxe5
28 Qa2+!	Rf7
29 Bxh5!	gxh5
30 Bxe5	Qxe5
31 Rd7	Qf5
32 Rxf7	Qxf7
33 Qd2	

33 Qxf7+ Kxf7 34 Rd1 would also have been sufficient.

33...	Re8

34 Rd1 Qg6 35 Qf4 Rf8 36 Qe3 Qf6 37 Kg1 Qf5 38 Qxa7 Qc2 39 Qd4 Rxf2 40 Qc4+ Rf741 Rf1 **resigns.**

#27. KASPAROV –McNAB
Dortmund (World Junior), 1980
1 e4 g6 2 d4 d6 3 Bg5!? Bg7 4 c3 Nf6 5 Nd2 Na6

Yes, the transpositional paths to the Torre even arise from 1 e4!

The plan with the couterattack involving c7-c5 supported by Na6 has a troubled history.

        6 Ngf3   0-0

We have now tranposed to the line under discussion.

        7 Be2   c5
        8 0-0   Nc7
        9 dxc5   dxc5
        10 Qc2   Ne6
        11 Bh4   Nf4
        12 Bc4!

The bishop escapes, and now the Nf4 looks pretty silly.

        12 ...   Qd7
        13 a4!

To prevent b7-b5.

        13...   N6h5

Or 13...a6 14 a5 ±.

        14 Rfe1   Qg4
        15 Bg3   e5
        16 Rad1

White calmly takes control of an important central file.

        16 ...   Qd7
        17 Nf1   Qc7
        18 Ne3

A bit of maneuvering has worked to White's benefit. His pieces are positioned effectively, while Black has not yet completed his development.

18 ...	Be6
19 Bxe6	Nxe6
20 Nd5	

Exploiting the critical weakness in the center.

20 ...	Qb8
21 Bh4!	

The resurrection of the cleric is a powerful one, dominating the kingside.

21 ...	Kh8
22 Nd2	b5
23 axb5	Qxb5
24 Ra1	Nhf4
25 Qa4!	

Black's weaknesses can be exploited in the endgame.

25 ...	Qd3
26 Rad1!	

A brilliant move, seeing through all the garbage on the d-file to the critical d7-square, which the rook will soon occupy.

26 ...	Nxd5
27 exd5	Qxd5
28 Nc4	

28...	Qb7
29 Rd7	Qb8
30 Be7	Re8
31 Red1	

White has achieved complete domination of the d-file, and the rest is easy.

| 31... | Bf8 |

32 Bf6+ Bg7 33 Bxg7+ Kxg7 34 Nd6 Rf8 35 Rb7 Qd8 36 Nxf7+- Qf6 37 Rdd7! Qf4 38 Qxf4 exf4 39 Ng5+ Kf6 40 Nxh7+ resigns.

#28. BRONSTEIN–GUFELD
Tallinn, 1981

1 Nf3 g6 2 d4 Nf6 3 Bg5 Bg7 4 Nbd2 d6 5 e4 h6 6 Bh4

The best retreat in this line, although 6 Bf4 can transpose if Black plays g7- g5, but there are then other plans available, aiming at e7-e5 with tempo.

6 ...	g5
7 Bg3	Nh5
8 c3	e6

Black can play 8...Nbd7 first, if he chooses, and then after 9

Nc4 he can play 9...e6.

9 Nb3!?

The knight often goes to c4, but this plan also makes a lot of sense.

9 ...	Nd7
10 Nfd2	Nxg3
11 hxg3	a5
12 a4	

White has control of the center and the queenside.

12...	0-0
13 Bd3	f5
14 Qe2	Nf6
15 f4!	gxf4
16 gxf4	Bd73
17 e5	Nd5
18 g3	

White's position is very solid, but Black has real weaknesses on the kingside, and no counterplay anywhere.

18 ...	Qe8
19 Kf2!	

If the king went to the queenside, then Black might have opened up the game.

19 ...	dxe5
20 dxe5	Bxa4

Did White hang a pawn? Hardly! He has something very clever in mind.

$$21\ Rxa4!!\qquad Qxa4$$
$$22\ Bb5$$

$$22...\qquad Qa2$$

Forced

$$23\ Bd7!$$

This is what Bronstein saw far in advance.

$$23\ ...\qquad Ra6$$
$$24\ Rb1\qquad Ne7$$
$$25\ Qc4$$

The pressure mounts at e6, while Black's forces are scattered.

$$25\ ...\qquad a4$$
$$26\ Nc5\qquad Qxc4$$
$$27\ Nxc4$$

An endgame, but on White's terms.

$$27\ ...\qquad Ra7$$
$$28\ Rd1!$$

Again, an admirable display of patience, taking control of an important file in the center before grabbing the Pe6.

$$28\ ...\qquad Rfa8$$

Black prepares to advance the a-pawn after kicking the horse.

29	Bxe6+	Kf8
30	g4	b5
31	Ne3	fxg4
32	f5!	g3+
33	Kg2!	

33 Kxg3 Bxe5+ followed by a4-a3 gives Black some chances.

33...		Nc6
34	Nd7+	Ke8
35	f6	Bf8
36	Nf5	Nd8

Ugly, but f7 mate was threatened.

37	f7+!	

Anyway!

37	...	Nxf7
38	Nf6 mate	

#29. OLAFSSON–MAKI
Gjovik, 1985
1 Nf3 Nf6 2 d4 g6 3 Bg5 Bg7 4 Nbd2 0-0 5 e4

Black can adopt the King's Indian formation without taking immediate action in the center, but this allows e2-e4 in one move and is good for White.

5	...	h6
6	Bh4	c5
7	dxc5!?	

7 c3 would be the standard plan, but it is actually not so easy for Black to recover his pawn here.

7 ...	Na6

7...Qa5 8 e5 Nd5 9 c4 and the Pe7 falls, with the Pc5 gaining further support.

8 Bxa6!	bxa6
9 0-0	Nh5

An ungainly move, but Black must put immediate pressure on the White queenside or face a juggernaut as the pawns advance.

10 Rb1

10 b4 Bxa1 11 Qxa1 comes into consideration, but there is no need to adopt sacrificial measures.

10 ...	g5

11 Ne1!	Nf4

Or 11...gxh4 12 Qxh5 ±.

12 Bg3	a5

Black intends to develop his bishop at a6.

13 Bxf4	gxf4
14 Nd3	Qc7
15 Nf3	Ba6
16 Qd2	Rab8
17 Rfc1	

White has an enormous advantage, with his perfectly coordinated pieces ready to support the advance of the queenside pawns.

17...	Bb7
18 Re1	Ba6
19 Nxf4	Qxc5
20 c3	Bc4
21 b3	Be6
22 e5	

Not only is the Bg7 cut off from the queenside, but more importantly the Black forces are unable to get back to the kingside to defend the monarch. After a few preliminary queenside gestures, White moves in for the kill.

22...   a4

23 Nd4 Rb6 24 Re3 Rfb8 25 b4 Qc4 26 a3 Qa2 27 Rb2 Qc4 28 Nh5 Bg4 29 Nxg7 Kxg7 30 Re4 resigns.

#30. LEIN–HERNANDEZ
Saint John, 1988

1 d4 Nf6 2 Nf3 g6 3 Bg5 Bg7 4 Nbd2 d5 5 e3 0-0

On 5...Bf5, White has the interesting reply 6 b4!?, e.g. 6...0-0 7 Be2 a5 8 b5 c5 9 bxc6 bxc6 10 0-0 Nbd7 11 Nh4! h6 12 Nxf5 hxg5 13 Nxg7 Kxg7 14 c4 e6 15 Qa4‡ Persitz - Kopylov, USSR 1976.

6 Bd3   Nc6

The deployment of the knight at c6 hinders Black's natural counterplay along the c-file.

7 c3

The immediate 7 0-0 would allow 7...Nb4.

7...   Re8

7...Qd7 is an odd-looking move, but in the only known example it worked out well, when combined with a rather interesting plan: 8 0-0 e5!? 9 Nxe5 Nxe5 10 dxe5 Ng4 The point of Qd7 was to break the pin in order to make this move possible. 11 Nf3 Re8 12 Be2 (12 Bc2 is probably a better plan, supporting e4 and perhaps sliding to b3 to increase pressure at d5.) 12...Nxe5 13 Bf4 Nxf3+ 14 Bxf3 c6 15 Re1 Qe7 16 e4 Premature, but Black was ready to play Bf5, which would have been less good if the bishop were at c2. 16...dxe4 17 Rxe4 Be6 with an equal game in

Cifuentes - Pacis, Malta Olympiad 1980.

8 0-0	h6
9 Bh4	Bf5?!
10 Bxf5	gxf5
11 Bxf6!	Bxf6

The weakness of Black's kingside cannot be repaired.

12 Kh1	e6
13 Ne1	Ne7
14 Nd3	Ng6
15 f4	b6

Black is seeking counterplay on the queenside, but White's position is too solid.

16 Rf3	h5
17 Rh3	h4

This was the only way to defend the h-pawn, but now it is exposed, despite having three defenders.

18 Ne5!

Well-timed! Getting rid of the invader will cost Black one of the h-pawn's guardians.

18 ...	Bxe5

18...Nxe5 19 dxe5 Be7 20 Nf3 Kg7 21 Qe1 Rh8 22 Qf2 c5 23 Rg1 with the idea g2-g4.

19 dxe5	Kg7
20 Qe2	Rh8
21 a4!	

With the Black pieces preoccupied on the kingside, White strikes at the other side of the board, inhibiting the advance of the Black pawns and keeping a4-a5 in reserve. But the real action remains on the kingside.

21...	Qd7
22 Nf3	c5
23 Qf2	Qe7
24 Rg1	Rh6
25 Qe1	Rah8

Black has put all of his power into the defense of the h-pawn, and both sides have evacuated the queenside. But now White launches a surprise attack.

26 b4!?	Qd7
27 Qa1!	

A wonderful move in the style of Rèti.

27 ...	Rc8
28 b5	a6?!

Black sees the coming threat of Rd1 and c4, or Rb1 and a5, but this reaction is not justified.

29 bxa6	Ra8
30 Qe1!	Qxa4

30...Qe7 31 g4 hxg3 32 Rxh6 Kxh6 33 Qxg3 and if the Rook grabs the Pa6, it will take a long time to get home to the kingside:

33...Rxa634 Qh3+ Kg7 35 Ng5 Qe8 36 Qh7+ Kf8 37 Qh8+ Ke7 38 Qf6+ Kd7 39 Nxf7 Ne7 40 Nd6 with the idea Rg7 +-.

31 Nxh4

Finally the pawn falls, and the king is further exposed.

31 ...	Qe4

Pinning the g-pawn, thus slowing White's attack.

32 Qg3	Rxa6
33 Qg5	Rh8
34 Rg3	Rh6

35 Qf6+ Kg8 36 Nxg6 Rxg6 37 Rxg6+ fxg6 38 Qxg6+

Kh8 39 Qh6+ Kg8

My guess is that Black lost on time here, but after Qxe6+ White wins easily. Resigns

#31. ZYSK–HERMESMANN
Bundesliga, 1987

1 d4 Nf6 2 Nf3 g6 3 Bg5 Bg7 4 Nbd2 d5 5 e3 0-0 6 Bd3 b6

This plan is too slow, as White can play e3-e4, either immediately or after 7 Qe2 Bb7.

    7 e4

7 Qe2 Bb7 8 e4 dxe4 9 Nxe4 Nbd7 10 0-0-0! with a good game for White in Mariotti - Tatai, Rome 1977.

7 ...	dxe4
8 Nxe4	Nbd7
9 0-0	

9 Qe2!? with the idea 0-0-0 comes into consideration.

9...	Bb7
10 Qe2	Nxe4
11 Bxe4	Bxe4
12 Qxe4	Nf6
13 Qe3	

Black has liquidated a number of pieces, but has conceded the center and has holes on the light squares of the queenside

13...	Rc8
14 Rfe1	Re8
15 Rad1	Qd5
16 b3 b5	

Black must prevent c2-c4, but he can't stop it for long.

17 Qd3	c6
18 c4	bxc4
19 bxc4	Qa5

Black is clearly worse, though he is by no means lost yet. The weakness of the pawn structure is compounded by the passivity of his pieces.

20 Rb1!	Rb8

20...Qxa2?? 21 Ra1 Qb2 22 Reb1 and it's goodbye, queen!

21 Bf4	Rxb1
22 Qxb1	Qa6
23 Qb3	

The exchange of rooks and control of the h2-b8 diagonal represent significant improvements in White's position.

23 ...	Nd7
24 h3	Nb6
25 d5!	Qc8

Otherwise d5-d6 might have been effective.

26 dxc6	Qxc6
27 Qb5!	Qc8

27...Qxb5 28 cxb5 would have been a very unpleasant endgame for Black.

28 c5	Nd5
29 Bg3	e6
30 c6	Nb6
31 Rd1	

Again White seizes the only open file.

31...	f6
32 c7!	e5

33 Qc6   Kf7

Now everything is set for a combinative finish.

34 Bxe5!! Re6

34...fxe5 35 Ng5+ Kf8 *(35...Kg8 36 Rd8 Rxd8 37 cxd8Q+ Qxd8 38 Qe6+ Kh8 39 Nf7+ Kg8 40 Nxd8+)* 36 Rd8 Rxd8 37 cxd8Q+ Qxd8 38 Ne6+ +–.

35 Qc2 Rxe5 36 Nxe5+ fxe5 37 Rd8 Qe6 38 c8Q Nxc8 39 Rxc8 Bh6 40 Rc7+ Kg8 41 Rxa7 resigns.

#32. MUSE–GROSZPETER
Kecskemet, 1990

1 d4 Nf6 2 Nf3 g6 3 Bg5 Bg7 4 Nbd2 d5 5 e3 0-0 6 Bd3 Nbd7

This is a very popular formation for Black.

7 0-0

This calm move is the most sensible plan.

7 ...   Re8

8 e4!

Black's plan is to play e7-e5, but he cannot do that until the pin is broken. Therefore Rf8-e8 is, temporarily, a waste of time, and so e3-e4 is fully justified.

8 ...	dxe4
9 Nxe4	Nxe4
10 Bxe4	c5
11 dxc5!	

11 c3 Qb6=.

11 ...	Qc7

White will be trying to exploit his queenside majority, and therefore he now further disrupts the enemy pawns.

12 c6!	bxc6
13 c3	Nc5
14 Bc2	Ba6
15 Re1	Rab8
16 Qc1!	

Both defending b2 and supporting the c1-h6 diagonal.

16 ...	e5
17 b4	Nd3

This gains the bishop pair, but removes a useful defender. 17...Ne6 was a more solid continuation.

18 Bxd3	Bxd3
19 Bh6	Bh8

19...Bxh6?! 20 Qxh6 f6 21 Re3 maintains excellent attacking chances, while Black's forces are out of play.

20 Qe3	Qd7
21 Rac1	e4
22 Nd2	Be5
23 Nb3	Qd6
24 g3	

Black has achieved a little counterplay, but his Bd3 is

immobile.

24 ...	f5
25 Nc5	Rb5
26 f4!	

The pawn at c3 is perhaps White's greatest asset, controlling the key squares at b4 and d4, allowing this crushing move which forced Black's resignation, as the pin along the crowded e-file costs Black a piece after 27 Nxd3 1-0.

#33. TSEITLIN–KURZ
Budapest, 1989

1 Nf3 Nf6 2 d4 g6 3 Bg5 Bg7 4 Nbd2 d5 5 e3 0-0 6 Bd3 c5

This is another common plan for Black. It is, in effect, a reversed Catalan, but the extra tempo is important, as it hinders the thematic e7-e5 break.

7 c3	Nc6
8 0-0	Qb6

This move can also be played on the previous move, but after 7...Qb6 8 Rb1 play simply transposes.

9 Rb1	Re8
10 b4	cxb4

10...cxd4 11 cxd4 a5 12 Qa4 Bd7 13 bxa5 Qxa5 14 Qxa5 Nxa5 was agreed drawn in Spassky - Gligoric, Moscow 1967.

11 cxb4	Bg4

11...a5! would transpose into the previous note.

12 h3	Bxf3
13 Qxf3	a5

The interpolation of the Bc8-g4xf3 maneuver changes the game considerably, and leads to a completely different type of pawn structure. Now White forces the win of the Pd5.

14	Bxf6	Bxf6
15	Qxd5	axb4
16	Ne4!	Red8
17	Qb3	

17 Nxf6+ exf6 18 Qb3 also looks reasonable, since 18...Ra3? is met by 19 Qxa3!

17 ...		Kg7?!

A rather pointless move, since Black is going to recapture with the pawn anyway.

18	Nxf6	exf6
19	Rfc1	Qa5

Again not 19...Ra3? 20 Qxa3! It is not difficult to imagine what sort of endgames can arise if the pieces come off!

20	Rb2	Rd7
21	Rc5	Qa3
22	Bb5!	Rd6
23	Bxc6	Rxc6
24	Qxa3	bxa3
25	Rxb7	Rxc5
26	dxc5	

White's passed pawn is decisive, since it is not easy for Black to go after the Pa2 until his king is in position to stop White from queening.

26...		Rc8
27	Rb5	f5
28	Kf1	Kf6
29	Ke2	Ke6

	30 Ra5	Rb8

Black strives for activity, now that his a-pawn is forfeit.

	31 Rxa3	Rb2+
	32 Kf3	Rc2
	33 Ra6+	Ke5
	34 c6	g5
	35 g4	fxg4+
	36 hxg4	Rc5
	37 Ra7!	

The most effective move.

	37 ...	Ke6

37...Rxc6 38 Rxf7 Rh6 39 Rf5+.

	38 c7	f5

39 gxf5+ Kxf5 40 Ra5!! resigns

#34. SCHANDORFF–S.POLGAR
rapid, 1989

1 d4 Nf6 2 Nf3 g6 3 Bg5 Bg7 4 Nbd2 d5 5 e3 0-0 6 Bd3 c5 7 c3 b6 8 0-0 Bb7

This is yet another Catalan reversed. White has many interesting plans here, but I prefer the one chosen by original thinkers Larsen and Basman.

9 Qb1!?

This is a very useful move. It supports both queenside activity and the center with the option of an early e3-e4.

	9 ...	Nbd7

10 b4!?

10 Re1 Qe8 (10...Re8 11 e4 dxe4 12 Nxe4± Basman - Savon, Harrachov 1967) 11 e4 dxe4 12 Nxe4 Nxe4 13 Bxe4 Bxe4 14

Qxe4 e6 may be slightly better for White, but Black's position was solid in Larsen - Gilden, US Open 1972.

>   10 ...   Qc8

10...c4 11 Bc2 Re8 and now:

a) 12 Ne5!? Nxe5 13 dxe5 Nd7 14 f4 with the idea Nf3-d4, e.g., 14...f6 15 exf6 exf6 (*15...Nxf6 16 f5 Ne4 17 Nxe4 dxe4 18 Bxe4 Bxe4 19 Qxe4 Bxc3 20 Rad1* looks much too dangerous for Black. or *15...Bxf6 16 Bxf6 Nxf6 17 e4 dxe4 18 Nxe4 Nxe4 19 Bxe4 Bxe4 20 Qxe4±*) 16 Bh4 Rxe3 17 Bf2 Re8 18 Bd4 should provide sufficient compensation, unless Black can free his game with f5, but even after 18...f5 19 Nf3 it still seems that there is sufficient compensation, given Black's bad bishop and the holes in the pawn structure, but Black controls the e-file, and this keeps the White queen from getting to the kingside easily;

b) 12 a4 e5 13 dxe5 Nxe5 14 Nxe5 Rxe5 15 Nf3 Re8 16 Qd1 Qc8 17 Bxf6 Bxf6 18 Nd4 with a roughly level game, Sherwin - Mednis, US Championship 1963.

>   11 a4   Re8
>   12 a5   c4
>   13 Bc2

White is forcing Black to weaken the queenside.

>   13 ...   bxa5
>   14 Rxa5   e5

The only possible source of counterplay.

>   15 Ba4!

This removes an important source of support for the e5 square.

>   15...   Re6
>   16 Bxf6   Bxf6
>   17 Bxd7   Qxd7

18 Nxe5   Bxe5
19 dxe5   f6

19...Rxe5 20 Nxc4 was perhaps missed by Black in her earlier calculations.

20 exf6   Rxf6
21 Qd1   Raf8

Black's attack is looking dangerous, but White has a stopper!

22 Ne4!   Rf5
23 Nc5   Qf7
24 Qc2   Ba8

25 Ra6! ±   d4

26 cxd4 Bxg2 27 Kxg2 Rxc5

and Black either resigned or lost on time (1-0).

#35. KHASANOV–LITVINOV
Minsk, 1985

1 d4 Nf6 2 Nf3 g6 3 Bg5 Bg7 4 Nbd2 c5 5 Bxf6 exf6

This cannot be recommended, since Black has no compensation for his weak pawns.

6 dxc5

6 Ne4 cxd4 7 Nd6+! Ke7 8 Qxd4 is even more effective, as

seen in Bellon - Medina, Torremolinos 1977.

6 ...	Na6	
7 Nc4	0-0	
8 e3		

Black has escaped immediate disaster, but his d-pawn is very weak.

8 ...	Nxc5
9 Qd5	Qc7
10 Nd6!	

Stifling Black's development. White has a clear advantage here.

10...	Rb8
11 Nd4	f5
12 Bc4	Ne4
13 Nxe4	fxe4
14 0-0-0!	

The pawn will wait - development keeps the pressure on!

14...	a6
15 Bb3	b5
16 Qxe4	Bb7
17 Qg4	Rbe8
18 Nf3	d5

The pawn was useless anyway.

19 Bxd5	Bxd5
20 Rxd5	Rc8
21 Qe4!	Qa5
22 Kb1	Rfe8
23 Qd3	Qb4
24 Qb3	Qg4
25 Rg5!	Qe4
26 Rd1	Rc4
27 Qd3	Qc6
28 Rd5	Rb4

The domination of the d-file is more important than the diagonal.

29 b3	Rg4

30 Rd6 Qc5 31 Rd8 Rxd8 32 Qxd8+ Bf8 33 g3 h6 34

Rd5 Qb4 35 Ne5 Re4 36 Nd7 resigns

#36. YUSUPOV–GORELOV
Moscow Championship, 1981
1 d4 Nf6 2 Nf3 g6 3 Bg5 Bg7 4 Nbd2 c5 5 Bxf6 Bxf6 6 Ne4 Bxd4 7 Nxd4 cxd4 8 Qxd4 0-0 9 Qd2

a) 9 0-0-0 is the more traditional move, but White doesn't seem to get very far with it: 9...Nc6 10 Qd2 d5! 11 Qxd5 Qc7! Here Black has sufficient compensation along the c-file. 12 Qc5 (*12 Kb1 Rd8!* or *12 Qb3 Qf4+ 13 Qe3 Qxe3+ 14 fxe3* amounts to pretty much the same thing.) 12...b6 13 Qc3 Qf4+! 14 Qe3 Qxe3+ 15 fxe3 Ne5 16 Nf2 Be6 17 g3 Rac8 was agreed drawn in Kovacevic - Stein, Zagreb 1972. Should Black have offered?

b) 9 c4 Nc6 10 Qd2 d6 11 Nc3 Be6 12 e4 looks like a good Maroczy Bind but Kasparov has shown that it lacks teeth: 12...Qb6! (*12...f5?! 13 exf5 Rxf5 14 Be2 Qb6 15 0-0 += -* Kasparov) 13 Be2!? (*13 Rd1?! Ne5! 14 b3 f5* was good for Black in *Spiridonov - Kasparov, Skara 1980*, because White could not play as in the line above: *15 exf5 Rxf5 16 Ne4! Raf8 17 Be2 Rf4⌐*) 13...Nd4 14 0-0 Rac8 15 b3 is evaluated as equal by Kasparov, but despite the bad bishop at e2, the hole at d5 and the lack of a Bg7 give White some hopes for the endgame.

9 ...	Nc6
10 0-0-0	

| 10 ... | Qa5 |

10...d5! would have transposed to (a) in the previous note.

11 Nc3	d6
12 h4	Be6
13 Kb1	Rac8
14 e4	

The game now looks a lot like a Dragon Sicilian, but without the powerful Bg7, Black's chances of survival are slim to none.

14...	f6
15 f4	b5
16 h5	g5
17 fxg5	Ne5
18 gxf6	exf6
19 Nd5!	Qxd2
20 Rxd2	Bxd5
21 Rxd5	

Black has too many pawn weaknesses.

21...	f5

22 exf5 Rxf5 23 Bxb5 Rf2 24 Rc1 Rc5 25 c4 Rxg2 26 Rxd6 Nf7 1-0.

#37. Lobron–Hunerkopf
West Germany, 1986

1 d4 Nf6 2 Nf3 g6 3 Bg5 Bg7 4 Nbd2 c5 5 Bxf6 Bxf6 6 Ne4 Qb6

6...Qa5+ 7 c3 Bxd4 is cute, but it leads to an unclear position whose consequences have not yet been fully explored: 8 b4 Bxc3+ 9 Nxc3 cxb4 10 Qd5! Qb6 11 Na4 Qa6 12 Nc5 Qa3 was played in Ionov - Livshutz, Leningrad 1963. Black has three pawns for the piece, but is severely underdeveloped and I think that White is for choice.

7 Nxf6+	Qxf6	8 c3	d6

8...cxd4 9 cxd4 can be played immediately, but there is no rush.

9 g3!?

Lobron's fianchetto plan is unusual, but in this case it seems well-motivated by the weakness of the h1-a8 diagonal.

9 ...	cxd4
10 Nxd4	Nc6
11 Bg2	Bd7
12 Qb3	

White is applying a classical attacking method on the white squares.

12 ...	Nxd4
13 cxd4	Qxd4
14 Qxb7	

This pawn structure is better for White.

14 ...	Rc8
15 0-0	Qb6
16 Rfc1!	Rxc1+
17 Rxc1	Qxb7
18 Bxb7	e5

Black cannot castle because White would then be able to infiltrate along the seventh rank.

19 Bd5!

White's advantage is obvious.

19...	Ke7
20 Rc7	a5
21 Bc6	Rd8
22 Ra7	Ke6
23 Bxd7+	Rxd7
24 Rxa5	

And the rest is easy:

24...   Rc7

25 Rb5 Rc1+ 26 Kg2 Ra1 27 a3 d5 28 Rb6+ Kd7 29
g4 f5 30 gxf5 gxf5 31 e3 Ra2 32 Kf3 Kc7 33 Rb4
Kc6 34 a4 Kc5 35 Rb5+ Kc6 36 b3 e4+ 37 Kg3 f4+ 38
Kxf4 Rxf2+ 39 Ke5 Rxh2 40 b4 Re2 41 Rxd5 Rxe3
42 b5+ Kb6 43 Rd6+ Kc7 44 Rd4 Kb6 45 Rxe4 Rg3
46 Kd5 Ka5 47 Rd4 Rg7 48 Kc6 Rg8 49 Rd7 Rc8+ 50
Rc7 Ra8 51 b6 Ka6 52 Rxh7 resigns.

#38. CHRISTIANSEN–BOUAZIZ
Szirak Interzonal, 1987
1 d4 Nf6 2 Nf3 g6 3 Bg5 Bg7 4 Nbd2 h6

There is nothing wrong with challenging the bishop early in the
game, but it does remove some flexibility from Black's plans.

5 Bh4   g5

The most aggressive plan.

a) 5...c5 6 c3 will transpose to positions considered earlier.

b) 5...d6 6 e3 g5 is a variation on the same theme: 7 Bg3 Nh5
8 Bc4! Now there is little point in stationing the bishop at d3, as f7
is weak. 8...e6 9 c3 Nxg3 10 hxg3 Nd7 11 Qe2 Qe7 12 0-0-0! a6
13 Nb3 c5 14 dxc5 dxc5 15 Bd3± Damjanovic - Bogdanovic,
Sarajevo 1969.

6 Bg3   d6
7 e4   Nh5
8 c3

Once again we see White in complete control of the center.

8 ...   e6?!

A very timid response.

9 Bd3   0-0
10 Ng1!?

White is so far ahead in development that Christiansen decides to redeploy his forces. If Black hesitates too long before capturing at g3, the bishop will be able to escape via f2.

10 ...	Nxg3
11 hxg3	e5
12 dxe5	dxe5
13 Qc2	

Black has permanent weaknesses on the kingside, for which the bishop pair is inadequate compensation, especially with the Bg7 blocked by the Pe5.

13 ...	Nd7
14 Rd1	Qe7
15 Ne2	Nc5
16 Bc4	Kh8
17 b4	Nd7

Perhaps Black should have tried 17...Ne6!?

18 Nf1!

Again, White has the luxury of extra time, and uses it to transfer the knight to a more effective post.

18 ...	Nf6
19 Ne3	a5
20 a3	c6
21 Nc1?!	

More repositioning of knights via the first rank, though this time it seems to be a bad idea. White might have considered 21 Nf5 Bxf5 22 exf5 axb4 23 axb4 with unclear consequences or 21 0-0 axb4 22 axb4 and perhaps White can make some progress on the d-file, for example 22...Be6 23 Bxe6 Qxe6 24 Rd2 Rad8 25 Rfd1 Rxd2 26 Rxd2 with the idea Nf5.

21 ...	Ng4
22 Nxg4	Bxg4
23 Be2!	

The point of Nc1.

23 ...	Be6

23...Bxe2 24 Qxe2 and the knight is much stronger than the enemy bishop.

24 g4?!

One usually doesn't place pawns on the same color as one's bishop, but this prevents the confining g5-g4 and in any event the outpost on f5 is secured for a knight should that prove useful. Still, it closes the kingside. 24 Nb3!? axb4 25 axb4 Ra3 26 Nc5 Rfa8 gives Black good counterplay so perhaps White should simply have castled.

24 ...	axb4
25 axb4	c5
26 bxc5	Qxc5
27 0-0	

Finally! White's advantage has slipped a bit and Black has some pressure along the c-file, but Bouaziz becomes a little too attracted by the Pc3.

27 ...	Rfc8
28 Qb2	

Here 28...Rc7 would have been very strong, but Black falls into the trap.

28 ...	Qxc3??
29 Rd8+	

and Black resigned because after 29...Kh7 30 Qxc3 he drops a rook.

CHAPTER THREE
1 d4 Nf6 2 Nf3 d6 3 Bg5

#39. JANOWSKI–CAPABLANCA
Havana, 1913

1 d4	Nf6
2 Nf3	d6

This approach is especially popular with those who favor the King's Indian or Old Indian as Black. It allows the Nf6 to be defended by Nbd7.

3 Bg5	Nbd7
4 e3	e5

A typical Old Indian strategy, but White will not play c2-c4, and this changes the nature of the struggle considerably.

5 Nc3	c6

5...Be7 might have been wiser, as the text weakens the Pd6.

6 Bd3	Be7
7 Qe2	Qa5

According to O.Bernstein, 7...Qc7 should have been played. The queen will eventually be driven back to that square anyway, and c7 is the natural square for the piece in the Old Indian.

8 0-0	Nf8
9 Rad1	

9 Bxf6 Bxf6 10 Ne4 Be7 11 dxe5 dxe5 12 Nfd2 was an alternative plan which might also have been effective, but on the other hand it would have involved parting with the bishop pair.

9 ...	Bg4
10 h3	Bh5
11 dxe5	dxe5

Now the question is, which piece goes to e4?

         12 Ne4!   **Nxe4**

12...0-0-0 13 Bxf6 gxf6 14 Ng3 Bg6 15 Nf5 ±.

         13 Bxe7   **Kxe7**

13...Nc3!? was a reasonable try.

         14 Bxe4   **Bg6?**

14...Ne6 15 Qc4 Qc5!= or 14...Bxf3!? 15 Qxf3 Qxa2 16 Qg3 Ng6 17 Bxg6 hxg6 18 Qxe5+ Kf8 19 Qc7! ±.

         15 Qc4!   **Ne6**
         16 b4   **Qc7**
         17 Bxg6   **hxg6**
         18 Qe4   **Kf6**

18...f6 19 Qxg6 Rh6 20 Qg3 and Black has no compensation for the pawn.

         19 Rd3.

Perhaps more precise was 19 h4!

         19 ...   **Rad8**
         20 Rfd1   **g5**
         1 c4!

White is going to nail down the d6-square, so Black will be forced to exchange rooks.

21 ...	Rxd3

21...b6 22 Rxd8 Rxd8 23 Rxd8 Nxd8 24 Qg4 Ne6 25 h4!
gxh4 26 Qxh4+ Kg6 27 Qe4+ Kf6 28 g4 and e5 is just too weak.

22 Rxd3	Rd8?

Better 22...g6, for reasons which will soon become clear.

23 Rxd8	Nxd8
24 h4!	

The same theme as in the previous note, though here, at least,
Black hasn't further weakened the queenside.

24 ...	gxh4
25 Qxh4+	Ke6
6 Qg4+	Kf6
27 Qg5+	

Capablanca had overlooked this check in his calculations back
at move 22.

27 ...	Ke6
28 Qxg7	Qd6
29 c5	Qd5
30 e4!	

The pawn cannot be captured because of the fork at g5, but the
important point is that the queen will be driven from its useful
post.

30 ...	Qd1+
31 Kh2	f6
32 Qg4+	Ke7

33 Nxe5!

This brings about an endgame in which White's two extra pawns are decisive.

33...   Qxg4

34 Nxg4 Ne6 35 e5 fxe5 36 Nxe5 Nd4 37 g4 Ke6 38 f4 a5 39 bxa5 Kd5 40 g5 Kxc5 41 g6 Nf5 42 Kh3 Kd5 43 Kg4 Ng7 44 Kg5 c5 45 Nd7 c4 46 Nb6+ Kd4 47 Nxc4 Kxc4 48 f5 Kd5 49 f6 Ne6+ 50 Kh6 resigns.

CHAPTER FOUR
1 d4 Nf6 2 Nf3 d5 3 Bg5

#40. DIZDAR–GELFAND
Halle, 1987
1 d4 Nf6 2 Nf3 d5 3 Bg5 Ne4

The Trompowski strategy is sometimes employed, but with the pawn at d5 rather than c5 Black has less counterplay than usual.

4 Bf4

This re.ply takes advantage of the fact that Black will not be able to play d7- d6

| 4 ... | c5 |

a) 4...Bf5 5 e3 e6 6 h3 h5 7 Be2 with the idea Nh2, g4.

b) 4...e6 5 Nbd2 Bd6 6 e3 Bxf4 7 exf4 Qd6 8 g3 Qb4 9 Bd3! Nxd2 10 Qxd2± Rakic - Tomovic, Belgrade 1966 is a classic case of good bishop vs bad bishop.

| 5 c3 | Qb6 |

a) 5...e6 6 e3 Nc6 7 Nbd2 Nxd2 8 Qxd2 Bd6 9 Bb5!± Mititelu - Szabo, Romania Championship 1965.

b) 5...Nc6 6 Nbd2 Bg4 7 e3 e6 is a reversed Slav. 8 Qb3! Qb6 9 Nxe4 dxe4 10 Nd2 cxd4 11 exd4 Qxb3 12 axb3 Bf5 13 Bb5± Phillips - Hollis, Oxford 1967.

| 6 Qb3 | cxd4 |

6...Nc6 7 e3 e6 8 Nbd2 f5 9 Nxe4! fxe4 10 Ne5 Bd7 11 Nxd7 Qxb3 12 axb3 Kxd7 13 Be2± Trifunovic - Duckstein, Varna Olympiad 1962.

| 7 Nxd4 |

7 Qxb6 axb6 8 Nxd4 looks appealing, but it may not be strong: 8...f6! 9 Nb5 Na6 10 f3 Nec5 11 N1a3 e5 12 Bg3 Be7 13 e4 dxe4 14 Nc4 Be6 15 Nxb6 Rd8 was better for Black in Kotov -

Law, London 1977. White might consider 8 cxd4!?

7 ...   Qd8

Perhaps this is not necessary - see previous note.

8 e3

White has comfortable development, but Black is going to be able to take the center. The question is, should he do so immediately?

8 ...   f6

Perhaps Black should attend to his development instead.

9 Bb5+!   Kf7

Not 9...Bd7 10 Ne6!

10 Bc7!!   Qxc7
11 Qxd5+   e6
12 Qxe4

Not only is the Black king exposed, but White has an extra pawn.

12 ...   e5
13 Nd2!   Qb6

13...exd4 14 Bc4+!

14 f4   Nc6
15 Nc4   Qc5

15...Qc7 16 Nxc6 bxc6 17 Bxc6 Rb8 18 0-0-0 ±.

16 b4	Qe7
17 Nxc6	bxc6
8 Bxc6	Rb8
19 Bd5+	resigns

#41. PANFILIONOK–ANDREYEV
Podolsk, 1990

1 d4 d5 2 Nf3 Nf6 3 Bg5 c5

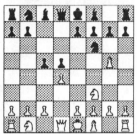

The Queen's Gambit reversed is a risky strategy, but play can often tranpose to lines previously considered.

4 Bxf6   gxf6
5 e3

5 Nc3 is a reasonable alternative, playing a Chigorin defense with an extra tempo.

5 ...   e6
6 c4!

This move is rarely appropriate in the Torre, but once Black has a shattered kingside, it is very effective.

6 ...   cxd4
7 exd4   Nc6
8 Nc3

Now the position resembles a reversed Tarrasch defense, with an extra tempo and more stable pawn structure for White.

8 ...   Bb4
9 Bd3   Qa5
10 0-0

White can afford to give up the pawn here - by analogy with the Cambridge Springs defense. This game features many opening flavors!

10 ...	Bxc3
11 bxc3	Bd7

11...Qxc3 12 cxd5 exd5 13 Qe2+ with the idea Rac1.

12 Qb3	dxc4
13 Bxc4	Qc7
14 Be2!	

The bishop gets out of the way so that the pawns can advance.

14...	0-0
15 d5	Ne7
16 c4	b6
17 Rad1	Ng6
18 Nd2!	

Aiming at e4, and forcing the following weakening move.

18...	f5
19 Rfe1	e5
20 Nf1	Qd6

Black attempts a blockading strategy.

21 Ng3	Nh4
22 Qc3	Rae8
23 Bf1	f6
24 Qd2!	f4
25 Ne4	

Black has succeeded in keeping the White queen out of the kingside, but allows the knight to reach its optimal post.

25...	Qe7

| 26 f3 | Nf5 |
| 27 Kh1 | Kh8 |

27...Ne3 28 Rxe3!? (*28 Rc1* is a safe and simple alternative, with the idea of advancing the c-pawn, as in the game) 28...fxe3 29 Qxe3 with compensation.

28 Rc1	Ne3
29 c5	bxc5
30 Nxc5	Qd6
31 Qa5!	Bf5
32 Ne4	Qxd5?

This leads to a simplification which gains material for White.

33 Qxd5	Nxd5
34 Nd6	Ne3
35 Nxe8	Rxe8
36 Rc7	

Black has insufficient compensation for the material.

36...	Rd8
37 Rxa7	Rd2
38 Kg1	Bc2
39 Rc1	f5
40 a4	e4
41 a5	Nd5
42 Rd7	e3

The advancing e-pawn is no match for the a-pawn, because White has better defenses.

| 43 Rxc2! | Rxc2 |

44 Rxd5 e2 45 Bxe2 Rxe2 46 Rxf5 Ra2 47 h4 Kg7 48 h5 Ra4 49 Kh2 Kh6 50 Kh3 Rb4 51 Kg4 Rb2 52 Kxf4 Rxg2 53 Ke5 Rd2 54 Ke6 Rd3 55 Rd5 Rxf3 56

Kd6 Kg7 57 Kc6 Kf6 58 a6 Ke6 59 Ra5 Rc3+ 60 Kb6
resigns

#42. OSKAM–EUWE
Holland, 1921

1 d4	Nf6
2 Nf3	d5
3 Bg5	

3 ...	Bg4

In this game we consider a few other moves for Black as well.

a) 3...h6 4 Bxf6 cripples Black's pawn structure without
compensation.

b) 3...Nbd7 4 c3 h6 5 Bxf6 Nxf6 6 e3 c6 7 Bd3 Be6?! 8
Nbd2 g6 9 Ne5 Bg7 10 f4 Nd7 11 0-0 Nxe5 12 fxe5 Qd7 13 Qf3
h5 14 Rae1 Bh6 15 Nb3 b6 16 e4! 0-0-0 17 exd5 Bxd5 18 Be4
with better prospects for White in Tipary - Rethy, Hungary
Championship 1955. If Black had castled kingside, White would
have launched a typical stonewall attack.

c) 3...Bf5 4 c4!? c6 5 Nc3 e6 6 cxd5 cxd5 7 e3 Be7 8 Qb3!
Qb6 9 Bb5+ Nc6 10 Ne5 Nd7 11 Nxd7 Kxd7 12 Bf4 h5

and now 13 Nxd5! brought White a winning game in Gasic -
Leylic, Sarajevo 1973.

d) 3...Nc6 4 e3 Qd6!? 5 Nbd2 Bf5 6 c3 Ne4 7 Bf4 Qd7 8 Bb5‡ Farwig - Herter, West Germany 1961. After castling, White will be able to play c4.

4 c4!

Whenever the Bc8 is prematurely developed, the Queen's Gambit strategy is most effective.

4 ...	e6
5 e3	h5?!

Hardly the move of a future world champion! Perhaps this was a typo for 5...h6.

6 Bxf6!	Qxf6
7 Qb3!	Nc6

7...b6 8 cxd5 exd5 9 Qxd5 ±.

8 Qxb7	Kd7
9 cxd5	

9 Qxa8? Bb4+ and then 10...Rxa8.

9 ...	exd5
10 Bb5	

and Black resigned, because of 10...Rc8 11 Bxc6+ Qxc6 12 Ne5+ Rxe5 13 Qxc6+ Kxc6 14 dxe5 etc.

CHAPTER FIVE
1 d4 Nf6 2 Nf3 c5 3 d5

#43. PIKET–J.POLGAR
Brussels–B, 1987

1 d4	Nf6
2 Nf3	c5

This choice by Black can radically alter the nature of the Torre, if White chooses to advance the pawn. This advance is recommended.

3 d5	b5

The most principled reply, preventing c2-c4 and gaining space on the queenside. But there are a number of less radical moves which will be considered in games cited below. This one is a a a quickie.

3...c4 is a strange reply from Buecker, who has given it the name HABICH (a short form of a German phrase meaning "gotcha"! But the following refutation is provided by Joel Benjamin, in our Unorthodox Openings book: 4 Nc3 Qa5 5 Nd2 b5 6 e4 d6 (6...e6 7 Be2!±) 7 a4 Ba6 8 axb5! Qxa1 9 Bxc4 Nxe4 (9...Qa5 10 bxa6 with compensation) 10 Ndxe4 Bb7 11 0-0 Nd7 12 Qe2 Ne5 13 Ba2 with the idea f4 ±. Buecker later tried to rehabilitate the line with 4...b5, but after 5 Qd4 Qa5 6 Nd2! Na6 7 e4 e6 he overlooked 8 d6! Nb4 (8...g6 9 Be2 Bg7 10 e5 or 8...Nb8 9 Qc5) 9 Kd1, as pointed out by Harding. Myers gives further 9...Nc6 10 Qc5 b4 11 Qxa5 Nxa5 12 Nb5 Rb8 13 Nc7+ Kd8 14 e5 Ng4 with the comment that 'Black survives his bisected position with advantage." Hardly. 15 Nf3 looks very strong: 15...Bxd6 (15...Nxf2+ 16 Ke1 Nxh1 17 Bg5+ f6 18 exf6 Bxd6 19 fxg7+ Kxc7 20 gxh8=Q) 16 exd6 Nxf2+ 17 Ke1 Nzxh1 18 Ng5 threatens mate, and on 18...Rf8, then 19 Nxh7 Rh8 20 Bg5+! f6 21 Nxf6, and the knight cannot be captured because of mate. If 22...Bb7 then 23 Nfd5+ Kc8 24 Ne7+ Kd8 25 Nc6++ Kc8 26 Nxa7 mate.

| 4 Bg5 | Qb6 |

4...d6 is considered a more reliable move, e.g., 5 e3 a6 6 a4 b4! 7 Bc4 Nbd7 8 Nbd2 g6 9 e4 Bg7 10 h3 0-0 11 0-0 Nb6 with an unclear position in Larsen - Browne, Hastings 1972/73.

| 5 a4 | bxa4?! |

This is generally a poor strategic choice, but it has the imprimatur of ECO. Black should probably advance the pawn, as in the previous note.

| 6 Nc3! |

An obvious, but powerful gambit which is much better than ECO's 6 Bxf6?!.

| 6 ... | Qxb2 |
| 7 Bd2 | Qb7 |

The threat was Rb1 followed by Nb5.

8 e4	g6
9 Rb1	Qc7
0 e5!	

In return for a couple of weak pawns White has a huge lead in development and absolute control of the center.

| 10 ... | Ng4 |
| 1 d6! | Qd8 |

11...exd6 12 Nb5 Bc3 exd6+.

12 Nd5	exd6
13 Bg5!	f6
14 exf6	

The idea is to play f6-f7.

| 14 ... | Qa5+ |
| 15 Nd2 | Ne5 |

16 Rb5　　　resigns

#44. KASPAROV–MILES
Hamburg (m/3), 1986

1 d4 Nf6 2 Nf3 c5 3 d5 b5 4 Bg5 Ne4

This is more in the spirit of the Trompowski.

5 Bh4

5 Qd3 Nxg5 6 Nxg5 h6 7 Nh7 is a simple alternative which also looks good for White, as suggested in ECO.

5 ...　　　Qa5+
6 Nbd2

Perhaps 6 c3 would be wiser.

6 ...　　　Bb7
7 a4　　　Bxd5
8 axb5

8 ...　　　Qc7

a) 8...Qxb5? 9 c4 Bxc4 10 Nxe4 Qxb2 11 Rc1 +-

b) 8...Qb6 9 Ra4! Nxd2? (9...Qb7 transposes to the game.) 10 Qxd2 ±

9 Ra4　　　Qb7
10 c4　　　Nxd2

11 cxd5	Nxf1

11...Nxf3+ 12 exf3 ±

12 Qd3!	

The knight is trapped anyway, so Kasparov defends the Pb5!

12 ...	d6
13 e4	Nd7

13...Nxh2 14 Nxh2! Nd7 15 0-0 g6 16 f4 Bg7 17 Nf3 ± is given by Braga.

14 Qxf1	h6

14...g6 15 Qe2 Bg7 16 0-0 Nb6 17 Ra3 0-0 is suggested by Braga.

14...Rb8 also comes into consideration and now:

a) 15 Nd2 Qxb5 16 Qxb5 Rxb5 17 Nc4 Rb4 18 Rxb4 cxb4 19 0-0 Nc5 20 f3 and White will quickly grab the a-pawn, since Black will need a lot of time to get his rook into the game. 20...g6 21 Ra1 a6 22 Be1 b3 *(22...Bg7 23 Bxb4 0-0 24 Bxc5 dxc5 25 Rxa6 Rb8 26 Ra7 ±)* 23 Bb4 Bg7 24 Bxc5 dxc5 25 Rxa6 0-0 26 Rb6 Bd4+ 27 Kf1 Ra8 28 Rxb3 Ra1+ 29 Ke2 Rg1 30 e5 Rxg2+ 31 Kd3 ±;

b) 15 Qe2?! Qxb5 16 Qxb5 Rxb5 17 Rxa7 is evaluated as ± by Braga, but I don't understand, since Black can just grab the b-pawn with 17...Rxb2.

15 Qe2	g5
16 Bg3	Bg7

16...Nb6 17 Ra3 Bg7 might have been wiser.

17 e5	0-0
18 h4	Qxd5
19 hxg5	

This is a complicated position, but Black could have equalized with the right move.

	19 ...	Nxe5?

19...hxg5! 20 Nxg5 Nxe5 21 Qh5 Qd3! 22 Re4 Qb1+ 23 Ke2 Qd3+ 24 Ke1 etc. would have given Black a draw.

	20 Bxe5!	dxe5 21 gxh6

Now Black is in a hopeless position.

	21 ...	Bf6	22 Rh5
	Kh8	23 Nxe5!	Qb3

23...Bxe5 24 Rxe5 Qb3 25 Rg4 e6 26 Rxc5 +–.

	24 Ra3	Qb4+

25 Kf1 Rad8 26 Nc6 Qxb2 27 Qxb2 Bxb2 28 Rxa7 Rc8 29 Rxe7 c4 30 Ke2 c3 31 Kd3 resigns

#45. PIKET–BOSBOOM
Amsterdam OHRA, 1988

1 d4 Nf6 2 Nf3 c5 3 d5 b5 4 Bg5 d6 5 e3 Nbd7

An interesting plan in which Black gives up a pawn for counterplay and avoids the doubling of pawns on the kingside.

	6 Bxb5	Qa5+
	7 Nc3	Rb8
	8 Qd3	a6
	9 Bc6	Rxb2

Black has regained the pawn, but the White bishops are very active.

	10 0-0	g6
	11 Bxf6!	exf6
	12 Nd2	

White's pieces are all involved in the game, while Black's sit passively.

12...	Rb8
13 Nc4	Qc7
14 Rab1	Rxb1
15 Rxb1	Kd8

15...Bg7 16 Nb6 0-0 17 Nxc8 Rxc8 18 Qxa6 ±.

| 16 Bxd7 | Qxd7 |

17 Nb6 Qa7 18 Nxc8 Kxc8 19 Na4 Be7 20 Rb6! Rd8 21 Rxa6 Qb7 22 Rb6 Qa7 23 Qb5 resigns.

#46. KASPAROV–BELYAVSKY
Candidates (m/9), 1983

1 d4 Nf6 2 Nf3 c5 3 d5 d6

A solid move which allows Black to adopt a Benoni formation. But White doesn't have to cooperate!

4 Nc3!	g6
5 e4	Bg7
6 Bb5+	

The simple 6 Be2 is also good.

| 6 ... | Bd7 |

6...Nbd7 7 a4 a6 8 Be2 0-0 9 0-0 leads to rich and unclear play.

7 a4	0-0
8 0-0	Na6
9 Re1!	

Here it is not advisable to capture at a6, as the pressure on the b-file will compensate for the pawn structure.

9 ...	Nb4
10 h3	e6
11 Bf4!?	e5

11...Bxb5 was recommended by some commentators, but Kasparov points out that this would lead to complciations favoring White after 12 Nxb5!.

a) 12...a6 13 Nxd6 Nh5 14 Nxb7 Qb6 15 Bd6! Qxb7 *(15...Rfc8 16 c3)* 16 Bxf8 Rxf8 17 c3 ± - Kasparov;

b) 12...exd5 13 Bxd6 dxe4 14 Bxf8 Qxf8 *(14...Qxd1 15 Raxd1 Rxf8 16 Ng5 Nxc2 17 Re2)* 15 Ng5 Re8 16 Nc3 with insufficient compensation for the exchange.

12 Bg5	Bc8

12...h6 13 Bxf6 Bxf6 14 Bxd7 Qxd7 15 Nd2 Be7 might have provided more counterplay, according to Kasparov.

13 Nd2	h6
14 Bh4	g5

Black decides to go for broke.

14...Qc7 15 Be2! Ne8 16 Nc4 f5?! 17 Nb5 Qd7 18 exf5 gxf5 19 Bh5 gives White very powerful pressure thanks to the bishops.

15 Bg3	g4?!

15...h5! 16 Be2 g4 17 Bh4! gxh3 18 g3! was given by Kasparov, and now Black has too many weaknesses on the kingside.

16 hxg4	Nxg4
17 f3	Nf6
18 Bh4	Kh8
19 Ne2	Rg8
20 c3	Na6
21 Ng3	

| 21 ... | Qf8 |

21...Bf8 22 Ndf1 Be7 would have provided stiffer resistance, according to Kasparov.

22 Ndf1	Nh7
23 Ne3	Bf6
24 Bxf6+	Nxf6
25 Ngf5	

After this infiltration Black is effectively lost, with White dominating the board . The rest is just a matter of technique for the future World Champion.

| 25... | Nh5 |

26 Kf2 Bxf5 27 Nxf5 Nf4 28 g3 Nh3+ 29 Ke2 Rxg3 30 Nxg3 Qg7 31 Rg1 Rg8 32 Qd2 resigns.

#47. KASPAROV–ILLESCAS CORDOBA
Madrid (rapid), 1989

1 d4	Nf6
2 Nf3	c5
3 d5	e6
4 Nc3	

This is a Franco-Indian (1 d4 e6 2 e4 c5 3 d5 Nf6 4 Nc3), a variation which has never enjoyed a good reputation.

| 4 ... | exd5 |

5 Nxd5	Nxd5
Qxd5	

Black has traded off some pieces but is left with a serious backward pawn.

6 ...	Nc6
7 e4	d6
8 Bc4	Be6
9 Qd3	Nb4
10 Bb5+!	Ke7

A rather bizarre solution. It is based on a tactical trick that does not bring the desired results. 10...Bd7 11 Bxd7+ Qxd7 12 Qc3! would prevent Black from fianchettoing his bishop, for excample 12...Be7 13 Qxg7 Nxc2+ 14 Kd1 Nxa1 15 Qxh8+ Bf8 16 Bh6 Qe7 17 Bxf8 Qxf8 18 Qxf8+ Kxf8 19 Kd2.

11 Qe2	Nxc2+
12 Qxc2	Qa5+
13 Bd2	Qxb5

Black has an extra pawn, but his pieces are not functioning efficiently, save for the queen which is nicely posted at b5.

14 Bc3!

This makes it even more difficult to develop the kingside.

14 ...	f6
15 a4	Qb3
16 Qe2	Qc4

16...Bc4 17 Qe3 with the idea Nd2.

17 Qe3	Kf7
18 Nd2	Qa6
19 f3	

Now the king will finally be able to shift position.

19...	g6
20 Kf2	Bg7
21 Rhd1	Rhe8
22 Qf4	Rad8
23 Nf1	

White still has strong pressure for the pawn, despite the fact that Black has developed and has the bishop pair. Black decides to eliminate the backward Pd6.

23 ...	d5
24 exd5	Rxd5
25 Nc3	g5?!

This creates a serious weakness on the kingside. 25...Rxd1 26 Rxd1 Qc6!? was better.

| | 26 Qc7+ | Re7? |

The Spaniard waves a red flag in front of Kasparov, who charges right at him!

27 Qxe7+!!

A brilliant move which secures the victory.

27 ...	Kxe7
28 Nxd5+	Kf7
29 Nc7	Qc4

30 Rd8

30 Nxe6 Qxe6 31 Re1 Qc6 32 a5 was a reasonable alternative.

30 ...	g4
31 Re1	Bf5
32 Ne8	Qxa4

33 Nxg7 gxf3

Or 33...Kxg7 34 Re7+ Kg6 35 Rf8 Qc2+ 36 Re2 +-.

34 Nxf5　　　Qc2+

35 Kxf3 Qxf5+ 36 Kg3 b5 37 Ree8 Qg5+ 38 Kf2 Qf4+ 39 Kg1 Qc1+ 40 Re1 Qc2 41 Rd6 f5 42 Rf6+ Kg8 43 Re8+ Kg7 44 Rxf5+ Kg6 45 Rf6+ Kh5 46 Re5+ Kg4 47 h3+ Kh4 48 Be1+ resigns

#48. ZYSK-SHORT
Bundesliga, 1987

1 d4 Nf6 2 Nf3 c5 3 d5 g6 4 Nc3 Bg7 5 e4 d6 6 Be2 0-0 7 0-0 Na6 8 Bf4 Nc7 9 a4 b6 10 Re1 Re8 11 h3 Bb7 12 Bc4 a6 13 Qd2 Nd7 14 Rad1

White has a significant advantage in space. Black's position is passive, and Short now radically changes the position in order to create counterplay.

14 ...　　　　　Ne5?!

This leads to a series of exchanges which brings about an inferior position for Black. The idea was that the light squares in the center would be placed under hypermodern pressure with an eventual e7-e6.

15 Bxe5	dxe5
16 d6!	

This short-circuits Short's plan, and Black is left with a bad bishop and a big hole at d5.

16 ...   exd6

17 Ng5!

17 Qxd6 Qxd6 18 Rxd6 is also very good for White, but Black does not have to exchange queens.

17 ...   d5!

The only practical way to guard f7.

18 exd5   h6
19 Nge4   Rb8

Black will try to arrange counterplay on the queenside, but White's domination of the center guarantees a significant advantage.

20 Ba2   Ba8
21 d6   Ne6
22 Nd5   Kh8

22...Nd4 is met by the simple 23 c3.

23 Ne7   Rb7?!

This ugly move is intended to prepare an exchange sacrifice at e7, But White moves too quickly on the kingside.

24 Bxe6!   fxe6
25 Nxg6+   Kh7
26 Ne7   c4

26...Rbxe7? 27 dxe7 Qxe7 28 Qd3 is clearly undesirable.

27 Qe2 ·   b5

    With Black's pieces tangled and their monarch undefended, White has the basis for combinatorial play.

28 Ng5+!

    and here Black resigned, because of 28...hxg5 *(28...Kh8 29 Nf7+)* 29 Qh5+ Bh6 30 Qg6+ Kh8 31 Qxh6+#.

CHAPTER SIX
1 d4 Nf6 2 Nf3 b5

The Polish defense is a playable alternative to the more common plans, but White can continue with the standard plan of Bg5.

#49. STEMPIN–WONG
Thessaloniki Olympiad, 1988

1 d4	Nf6
2 Nf3	b5
3 Bg5	

3 ...	Bb7

a) 3...d5 4 e3 c6 5 Nbd2 h6 6 Bh4 Bf5 7 Bd3! Bxd3 8 cxd3 Nbd7 9 Rc1 Qb6 10 0-0 e6 11 Bxf6 gxf6 12 Qc2 Rc8 13 e4± Wirthensohn - Partos, Biel 1977.

b) 3...Ne4 4 e3! a6 5 Bh4 d5 6 Nbd2 Bf5 7 Nxe4 Bxe4 8 Bd3 Bg6 9 a4± Kozlov - Gurgenidze, Rostov on Don 1976.

4 e3	a6
5 Bd3	e6

5...g6 6 Nbd2 Bg7 7 c3 0-0 8 e4±.

6 Nbd2	c5
7 c3	d5
8 Ne5	Nc6
9 f4	

White has a favorable stonewall formation and Black is saddled with a bad Bb7.

9 ...	h6
10 Bh4	Be7
1 0-0	Qc7
12 a3	0-0
13 Qf3	c4
14 Bc2	Ne4

A desperate attempt to obtain some active play, but White reacts correctly.

15 Nxe4	Bxh4
16 Ng3!	Bxg3

16...Be7 17 Qh5! with tremendous pressure.

17 hxg3	Nxe5
18 fxe5	Qe7
19 Rf2	f6
20 Raf1!	Bc6

20...f5 21 g4 fxg4 22 Qxf8+! Rxf8 23 Rxf8+ Qxf8 24 Bh7+ wins, according to H. Myers. Or 20...f5 21 g4 g6 22 gxf5 gxf5 23 g4, also accoring to Myers.

21 g4	a5
22 g5!	f5
23 gxh6	Qg5

23...gxh6 24 Qh3 Qg5 25 Rf3 ±.

24 hxg7	Rf7
25 g4	Rxg7
26 Rg2	fxg4
27 Qf4!	

The Pg4 can be picked up later.

27...	b4
28 Qxg5	Rxg5
29 Rf4	bxa3
30 Rgxg4	Rxg4+
31 Rxg4+	Kf7
32 bxa3	

In this endgame, the better bishop wins.

32...	Rb8
33 Rg2	Kf8
34 Rf2+	Ke7
35 Kg2	Be8
36 Kg3	Rb2
37 Bd1	Rb1
38 Bg4	Rb3
39 Rh2!	Bg6

39...Rxc3 40 Rh7+ Kf8 41 Bxe6 Rxe3+ 42 Kf2 Rxa3 43 Bxd5 c3 44 Rc7 Ba4 45 Be4 Ra2+ 46 Ke1 c2 47 Kd2 ±.

40 Rh6	Kf7
41 Kf4	Rxc3
42 Kg5	Be4
43 Bxe6+	Kg7
44 Rf6	Rc1

44...Rxe3 45 Rf7+ Kh8 46 Kh6!+-.

45 Rf7+	Kh8

46 Rf8+ Kg7 47 Rf7+ Kh8 48 Bg4 Rg1 49 e6 Kg8 50 Rf6 c3 51 e7 Bg6 52 Rxg6+ Kf7 53 Rg7+ resigns.

CHAPTER SEVEN
1 d4 Nf6 2 Nf3 b6

#50. C.TORRE–VERLINSKY
Moscow, 1925

1 d4	Nf6
2 Nf3	b6
3 Bg5	Bb7
4 Nbd2	

This structure can be handled in a number of ways by Black, most of which will transpose into other lines. Verlinsky chose to overprotect the e4-square.

4 ...	d5
5 e3	Nbd7
6 Bd3	e6
7 Ne5!	

Taking advantage of the fact that Black cannot afford to capture, White establishes a strong outpost at e5, which can be supported by an advance of the f-pawn.

7 ...	a6

7...Nxe5? 8 dxe5 h6 9 Bh4 g5 10 exf6 gxh4 11 Qf3 is crushing, since Black has no knights to go after the Pf6.

8 f4	Be7
9 0-0	c5
10 c3	

White has achieved a superior stonewall formation, with a "liberated" bishop.

| 10 ... | 0-0 |
| 11 Qf3 | Nxe5 |

Black has run out of useful waiting moves.

| 12 fxe5 | Nd7 |
| 13 Qh3! | |

The attack is already dangerous.

| 13 ... | g6 |
| 14 Bh6 | c4?! |

In one sense, the move is merely irrelevant, since it does not address the kingside threats. But even if White didn't come up with an inspired attack the Bb7 would be a spectator forever. Naturally, there is no reason for White to capture at f8.

15 Bc2	b5
16 Rf2	Qb6
17 Raf1	f5

Pretty much forced.

| 18 exf6 | Rxf6 |
| 19 Nf3! | |

All of White's pieces are participating in the attack, while most of Black's are off vacationing on the queenside.

19 ...	Re8
20 Qg3	Nf8
21 Ne5	

Returning to the favored outpost

| 21 ... | Qd8 |
| 22 h4 | |

The threat of h5 is so strong that Black tries to give up the exchange to reduce the pressure at g6.

22 ...	Rf5
23 Bxf5	Bxh4

24 Bxg6!!

A brilliant finish to a well-conducted attack.

24 ...	Bxg3
25 Bf7+	Kh8
26 Bxe8	Bxf2+
27 Rxf2	resigns

CHAPTER EIGHT
Double Fianchetto for Black

#51. PETROSIAN–WADE
Leipzig Olympiad, 1960

1 d4 Nf6 2 Nf3 b6 3 Bg5 Bb7 4 Nbd2 g6 5 e3 Bg7 6 Bd3

Black has chosen to fianchetto both of his bishops, a plan which has the usual drawback of making it difficult to play in the center.

6 ...	c5
7 c3	d6

Taking the e5-square away from the Nf3.

8 0-0	0-0
9 Qc2	h6

9...Nbd7 10 Rfd1 Qc8 11 a4 Qc7 12 a5 e5? gave White a better game in Trifunovic - Teschner, Dortmund 1961.

10 Bh4	Nbd7

10...g5 11 Bg3 Nh5?! 12 Nxg5! Nxg3 13 fxg3 hxg5 14 Qh5 f5 15 Rxf5 wins for White.

11 h3	Nh5
12 Nh2	cxd4
13 cxd4	Bf6

An interesting decision, and probably a wise one. Even though the Black parts with an important defender, he eliminates annoying kingside pressure.

14 Bxf6	Ndxf6
15 Rac1	Rc8
16 Nhf3	Rc7

16...Ng7!? comes into consideration.

17 Nb3

In order to overprotect c1 and allow the exchange of rooks.

17 ...   Rxc1

18 Rxc1   Qa8!

Black's position is now fully equal, but a fascinating endgame lies ahead.

19 Ba6   Rc8

19...Bxf3 20 Qxf3 Qxf3 21 gxf3 is better for White, since the powerful bishop makes up for the pawn structure, and the weakness at h3 is particularly hard to exploit. Moreover, White has control of the only open file.

20 Rxc8+   Bxc8

21 Nbd2

Not 21 Qc4? Bxh3!

21 ...   Qc6

22 Bxc8   Qxc8

23 Qc4   Qxc4

24 Nxc4   Nd5

25 Kf1   Nhf6

26 Ke2

White effectively exploits the fact that Black must take time to get his knights back into the game. The centralized king is a definite advantage, and Black will soon have to spend time to emulate it.

26...   Kf8

27 Ne1!   Ke8

28 Nd3   Kd7

29 f3   Nc7

30 e4

White now has firm control of the center and enjoys a

significant advantage, though Black's game is by no means hopeless.

| | 30 ... | Nfe8 |

30...e6? 31 e5 Nfe8 (*31...dxe5 32 Ndxe5+ Ke7 33 Nc6+*) 32 exd6 Nxd6 33 Nde5+ Ke7 34 Nxd6 Kxd6 35 Nxf7+ Kd5 36 Nxh6 Kxd4 37 Nf7 ±.

| | 31 h4 | f6? |

31...Ne6 was necessary. Now White pins down the Black pieces and quashes all counterplay.

| | 32 d5! | c6 |

32...f5 33 exf5 gxf5 34 Ne3 Nf6 35 Nf4 e6 36 dxe6+ Nxe6 37 Nxe6 Kxe6 38 Kd3 and the superior pawn structure gives White all the chances.

	33 dxe6+	Nxe6
	34 Ne3	g5
	35 Nf5?!	

Better was 35 h5.

| | 35 ... | h5! |
| | 36 Ke3 | N8g7 |

36...N8c7! was the right direction for the horse, e.g., 37 hxg5 fxg5 38 f4 d5! 39 Ne5+ Ke8 40 fxg5 Nxg5 41 Ng7+ Kf8 42 Nxh5 Nxe4 =.

	37 Nxg7	Nxg7
	38 hxg5	fxg5
	39 f4	

| | 39 ... | gxf4+? |

39...Ne6! would have saved the game: 40 fxg5 Nxg5 41 Nf4 h4 42 Kd4 Kc6 43 e5 dxe5+ 44 Kxe5 Kc5 45 Kf5 Nf7 46 Ng6 Kd4 47 Nxh4 Kd3 48 g4 Nh6+ 49 Kg5 Nxg4 50 Kxg4 Kc2 and the monarch munches the pawns.

40	Nxf4	Ke7
41	Kd4!	Kf6

Now Petrosian gives a good endgame lesson!

Note that 41...Ne6+ loses to 42 Nxe6 Kxe6 43 g3!+–.

42	Kd5	Kg5
43	Ne2!	Ne8
44	Kc6	Nf6
45	Kb7	Nxe4
46	Kxa7	Kf5

The king just can't find a way into the kingside!

47	Kxb6	Ke5
48	a4	d5
49	a5	d4

50	Nxd4	Kxd4
51	Kc6!	Nc5
52	b4	Nd3

52...Na6 53 b5 Nb8+ 54 Kc7 Kc5 55 a6!

53	Kb5!	Ke5

53...Nf4 54 a6 Nd5 55 a7 Nc7+ 56 Kc6 Na8 57 Kb7.

54	a6	Nxb4

and Black resigned without waiting for White's reply.

CHAPTER NINE
1 d4 d5 2 Nf3 e6 3 Bg5

#52. YE RONGGUANG–VAN RIEMSDIJK
Manila Interzonal, 1990

1 d4	e6
2 Nf3	d5
3 Bg5	

The Torre Attack is even playable against this move order!

3 ...	Be7
4 Bxe7	Qxe7
5 c4	

We now have a Queen's Gambit with the dark-squared bishops off the board, and this favors White, whose light squared bishop will have more scope.

5 ...	Qb4+
6 Qd2	Qxd2+
7 Nbxd2	

The advantage remains in the endgame.

7...	Nf6
8 Rc1	c6
9 e3	Ke7
10 Bd3	Rd8
11 Ke2	Nbd7
12 a3	b6
13 cxd5	cxd5
14 Ne5!	

An important move, based on a correct assessment of the position.

14 ...	Nxe5

Otherwise 15 f4 would consolidate White's advantage.

15 dxe5	Ne8

15...Nd7 16 f4 Nc5 17 Bb1! a5 18 g4 ±.

16 Nf3	h6
17 Nd4	Bb7
18 f4	

White is in no hurry to occupy c6. The knight is very well placed at d4.

18 ...	Rac8
19 Kd2!	

This insures that the only way to contest the c-file will be to exchange both pairs of rooks, but that would lead to a lost endgame for Black.

19 ...	a6
20 g4	Rxc1
21 Rxc1	Rc8

This effectively concedes the game, but Black's position was hopeless anyway.

22 Rf1	

White would also stand well after the exchange of rooks, but the f-file is even more important.

22...	Nc7
23 f5	Rg8
24 h4	Ne8
25 fxe6!	fxe6
26 Bg6	

and Black resigned, because of 26...Nc7 28 Rf7+ Kd8 29 Nxe6! Nxe6 30 Rxb7.

CHAPTER TEN
1 d4 d5 2 Nf3 (Others)

#53 HORT–Z.POLGAR
Biel, 1987

1 d4	d5
2 Nf3	c5

This is a move which indicates that Black is comfortable playing a standard Queen's Gambit a tempo down.

3 dxc5

Why not accept the gambit, given that White enjoys an extra tempo? 3 c4 is often recommended, but given the viability of the Tarrasch defense, Black can simply play 3...e6, reaching normal lines.

3 ...   e6

a) 3...Nf6 4 c4! e6 5 cxd5 exd5 6 Be3! forces Black to take a lot of time regaining the pawn: 6...Na6 7 g3 Bxc5 8 Bxc5 Nxc5 9 Bg2 0-0 10 0-0 Bf5 11 Nc3 Re8 12 Nd4 Bg6 13 Bh3! and the control of the light squares (f5,c8) gives White a clear advantage, Alekhine - Kaufman, Odessa 1919.

b) 3...Qa5+ 4 Nbd2 Qxc5 5 e3 Nc6 6 a3± - Euwe White will be able to expand on the queenside with impunity.

4 Bg5!?

An interesting approach which may be more promising than the usual advance of the e-pawn, though White can continue in Queen's Gambit fashion, e g., 4 e3 Bxc5 5 Be2 Nf6 6 0-0 0-0 7 a3 b6 8 b4 Bd6 9 Bb2 Bb7 10 Nbd2 Nbd7 11 c4! Qe7 12 cxd5 Bxd5 13 Nd4 a5 14 b5 Nc5 15 Bf3 Nd3 16 Bxd5 Nxb2 17 Qb3 Nxd5 18 Qxb2 The position is roughly level, but White does control some important territory on the queenside and in this game managed to turn it into victory: 18...Qf6 19 Rac1 Rac8 20

Qb3 Qh6 21 g3 Bc5 22 N2f3 Qh5 23 Kg2 Nf6? A waste of time, since the knight will have to return to seal the d-file 24 Nc6 Kh8 25 Rfd1 h6 26 Rc4! Nd5 27 Rh4 Qg6 28 Nce5 Qh7 29 e4 Ne7 30 Rd7 Rce8

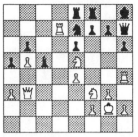

31 Ng5! Qg8 32 Qc3 f6 33 Rxe7! and in Janowski - Berger, Carlsbad 1907 Black resigned because 33...fxg5 34 Rxh6+! gxh6 35 Ng6 mate.

4 ...	f6
5 Bd2	Bxc5
6 c4	Ne7

6...dxc4 7 e3 b5 8 a4 and White will regain his pawn, while the a2-g8 diagonal will be a significant problem for Black.

7 e3	0-0
8 Nc3	Nbc6
9 cxd5	Nxd5

9...exd5 10 Rc1 and White can develop a dangerous attack with Bf1-d3-b1, though 10...Bf5 might be playable.

10 Qb1

10 Rc1 Ndb4 exploits the weakness at d3.

| 10 ... | f5?! |

Although Black is concerned about the b1-h7 diagonal, this move weakens a lot of squares.

11 Be2	Qe7
12 0-0	Nxc3
13 Bxc3	e5
14 b4!	

White is gaining space on the queenside, and the Black pawns will require constant protection.

| 14 ... | Bd6 |

14...Bxb4 15 Bxb4 Nxb4 16 Nxe5 Qxe5 17 Qxb4 with the idea Bf3.

15 b5	Nd8
16 Qb2	Nf7

The mounting pressure forces Black into a very artificial formation. White now has a clear advantage.

17 Rfd1	Bd7
18 Bc4	Be6

| 19 Bd5! | e4 |

19...Bxd5 20 Rxd5 Rfe8 21 Rad1 Rad8 22 a4 leaves Black with little to do, since all of his pieces are tied down.

| 20 Bxe6 | Qxe6 21 Nd4 |

21 Bxg7?! exf3 22 Bxf8 Be5! 23 Qb3 Qxb3 24 axb3 Bxa1∓.

21 ...	Qh6
22 h3	Ng5

Black has taken the initiative on the kingside, but has permanent weaknesses which White immediately exploits.

          23 Qb3+   Kh8
          24 Ne6!   Qxe6

24...Nxe6 25 Rxd6 Rae8 26 Rad1 and again Black is very restricted.

          25 Qxe6   Nxe6
          26 Rxd6   Nc5
          27 Bd4

The Rd6 controls both d7 and e6, so that the Nc5 is stranded.

          27 ...   Rac8

27...Nd3 28 Rd7 is obviously undesirable.

          28 Rc1   Nd3
          29 Rxc8   Rxc8
          30 Rd7   h5

Black is already lost. For example: 30...Rg8 31 Rxb7 f4 32 Rxa7 fxe3 33 fxe3 +-.

          31 Rxg7   Rc1+
          32 Kh2   Rf1
          33 Rf7+   Kg8
          34 Rxf5   h4
          35 Rh5   Rxf2
          36 Rxh4   Rxa2
          37 Rxe4

All pretty much forced, but Black has no compensation for the pawns.

          37...   a5

38 h4 Ne1 39 Rg4+ Kh7 40 Kh3 a4 41 Rg7+ Kh6 42 g4 a3 43 Rxb7 Re2 44 Rb6+ Kh7 45 g5 Rg2 46 Rh6+

Kg8 47 g6 Rh2+ 48 Kg4 resigns

#54. PORTISCH–LARSEN
Montreal, 1979

1 Nf3	d5
2 d4	Bf5

This defense enjoys partisan support at many levels of play, and is by no means unplayable, especially if White plays Nf3 before c4. Even in the present game, Black gets a reasonable position before going astray.

3 c4

3 Bg5!? might be playable, intending to capture on f6 if Black plays 3...Nf6.

3 ...	e6
4 Qb3	Nc6
5 c5	

5 Bd2 is a reasonable alternative.

5 ...	Rb8
6 Bf4	h6
7 e3	g5
8 Bg3	Bg7
9 Nc3	a6?!

9...Nge7! would have secured equality.

10 h4	g4
11 Ne5	Nge7
12 Nxc6	Nxc6
3 Be2	0-0
14 Qd1	

14 0-0-0 is an aggressive alternative.

14 ...   e5?!

The slow openings like the Torre Attack and the present game require patience, and that is not one of Larsen's strong points. 14...h5 was called for.

15 dxe5	d4
16 exd4	Nxd4
17 0-0	Qd7
18 Bc4	Bc2
19 Qc1	Rbd8
20 Re1	Bh7

Black has created some threats, but the kingside is still vulnerable. That is why White should have played the knight to the center here.

21 Bd5?!

21 Nd5! Nc2 22 Nf6+ Bxf6 23 exf6 Nxe1 24 Qxh6 +-.

21...	Qe7
22 Be4	Qxc5
23 Bxh7+!	Kxh7
24 Qf4	

The weakness of the kingside is still critical.

24...	Qb6
25 Rad1	Qxb2
26 Rxd4!	Qxc3
27 Rde4	Kh8
28 Qxg4	

Although the material is even, White has all the chances here.

28...	Rd4
29 Rxd4	Qxe1+
30 Kh2	Qa1

30...Bxe5?! 31 f4! Qxg3+ 32 Qxg3 Bxd4 33 f5 should be a pretty simple win.

| 31 Rd7 | Qxa2 |
| 32 Rxc7 | b5 |

32...Qd5 33 Rd7 Qb5 34 f4 a5 35 h5! a4 36 Bh4 a3 37 Bf6 Bxf6 38 exf6 Rg8 39 Rd8!

| 33 f4 | Qd5 |

34 Rd7	Qe4
35 Qh5	Kg8

35...b4 36 f5 b3 37 f6 b2 38 c6! b1Q 39 fxg7+ Kxg7 40 Be5+ Kh7 41 Rxf7+ Kg8 *(41...Rxf7 42 Qxf7+#)* 42 Rg7+ Kh8 43 Qxh6+ Qh7 44 Rxh7+.

36 Re7	Qb4

Neither 36...b4 37 f5 b3 38 e6 nor 36...Qd5 37 f5 Qc5 38 Qg4 Qxe7 39 f6 hold out any chances for survival.

37 Ra7	Qc5
38 Rxa6	b4
39 Qf3	Qb5
40 Ra7	Rb8
41 f5	

This move was sealed after 35 minutes of thought, but it didn't take long to finish it off when the game was resumed.

41...	Bxe5
42 f6	Kh8
43 Rxf7	Re8
44 Qg4	Bxg3+
45 Kh3!	

and Black resigned, not wanting to face 45...Rg8 46 Qe4. [Notes after Tal]

#55. STEINITZ–CHIGORIN
World Championship (m/2), 1889

1 Nf3	d5
2 d4	Bg4

This move is often played by those who enjoy the Black side of the Chigorin, which can arise after 3 c4 Nc6!?

3 Ne5!

Though Steinitz turned to 3 c4 for later games in the match, this move is logical One can compare lines in the Trompowski Attack (1 d4 Nf6 2 Bg5) where Black often plays an early Ne4.

3 ...	Bh5

3...Bf5 4 c4 f6 5 Nf3 e6 6 Qb3! b6 7 Nc3 c6 8 a4 Na6 9 cxd5 exd5 10 e4! dxe4 11 Bxa6 exf3 12 0-0 was clearly better for White in Lasker – Schiffers, Nurnberg 1896.

4 Qd3

This threatens 5 Qb5+!

4 ...	Qc8
5 c4	f6
6 Nf3	e6
7 Nc3	

White's natural development and control of the center constitute a tangible advantage.

7 ...	Bg6
8 Qd1	c6
9 e3	Bd6
10 Bd2	Ne7
11 Rc1!	

Black's artificial queen placement is exploited by the distant opposition of the White rook.

11 ...	Nd7

12 Nh4!

12 Be2 would have allowed 12...Bh5.

12 ...	f5
13 g4!	

White correctly determines that pressure at f5 will be an effective plan.

13 ...	Nf6
14 h3	Ne4
15 Bd3	fxg4

15...0-0 comes into consideration, threatening to cause problems at f3, for example 16 gxf5 Nxf5 17 Bxe4 dxe4 18 Nxg6 hxg6 19 Qg4 ±.

16 Nxg6	Nxg6

17 Bxe4!

Taking advantage of the opportunity to wreak havoc in the center.

17...	dxe4
18 Nxe4	Be7
19 hxg4	e5
20 d5!	

White has an extra pawn and Black has no counterplay whatsoever.

20...	Qd7
21 Bc3	Rd8
22 Rh5!	cxd5
23 cxd5	0-0
24 d6!	Qe6

24...Bf6 25 Rf5 ±.

25 Qb3	Qxb3
26 axb3	Bxd6
27 Nxd6	Rxd6
28 Bb4	Rb6
29 Bxf8	Kxf8
30 Rc8+!	Kf7
31 Rc7+	Kf6
32 Rf5+	

32 Rxh7 Rxb3 33 Rhxg7 Rxb2 34 Rxb7 Rxb7 35 Rxb7 Kg5 would have been more difficult for White.

32...	Ke6
33 Rff7	Rb4
34 Rxb7	Rxg4
35 Rxg7	

By preserving the b-pawn, White keeps his task simple.

35...	h5
36 Rxa7	Kf5
37 f3	Rg2
38 Ra6	

and Black resigned, since White can trade off all the pieces and win the pawn endgame.

OVERVIEW OF VARIATIONS

NOTES

NOTES

NOTES

NOTES